Dyslexia. Wrestling with an Octopus

For Harry, my special treasure

DYSLEXIA
Wrestling with an Octopus
10 Tips to Help Your Child
Thrive in Every Aspect of Life
Academically, Socially & Physically

Beth Beamish

Illustrations by Sarah Pitts

MERITS PUBLISHING

Dyslexia. Wrestling with an Octopus is one mother's guide to ten tips that have helped her son. This is not a one-size-fits-all approach and it is important to know your child's individual learning challenges.

As of press time, the URLs displayed in this book refer to existing websites on the Internet. Merits Publishing is not responsible for, and should not be deemed to endorse or recommend, any website other than its own, or any content available on the Internet (including without limitation, any website, blog post, information page) that is not created by Merits Publishing. The author is not responsible for third party material. Names have been changed in places to protect the individual's privacy.

Scriptures quoted are from the Good News Bible © 1994 published by the Bible Societies/HarperCollins Publishers Ltd UK, Good News Bible© American Bible Society 1966.

978-0-473-52191-2 - Softcover
978-0-473-52192-9 - Epub
978-0-473-52193-6 - Kindle

Contents

Introduction   11

And to think I saw it on Molesworth Street

How I discovered I had dyslexia and why you need this book.

Chapter One   19

The shape of me (and my dyslexia)

Why it is important to be aware of the health and social issues

that often accompany dyslexia.

Chapter Two   25

Bunches of hunches. Does my child have dyslexia?

How to spot dyslexia and what to do if you suspect your child

has it.

- Welcoming Harry to our family
- What is dyslexia?

- The dyslexia octopus
- Signs of dyslexia in young children
- Types of dyslexia
- Differences in the dyslexic brain
- Left brain and right brain tasks
- Why get an assessment for dyslexia?
- At what age should I get my child assessed?

Chapter Three 48

Harry hears a Who, but has no idea it starts with the letter 'W'

Learning challenges and what you can do to tackle them.

- Key early years' issues
- The impact of ear infections
- Key overlaps between dyslexia and glue ear (otitis media)
- The impact of speech difficulties
- The role of eye tracking difficulties and Irlen Syndrome
- The role of memory
- Working memory
- Processing speed
- The role of sleep
- Spelling and reading interventions
- Be your child's advocate
- Private tutors
- The Steps Programme

- Davis Dyslexia Correction Programme
- Fast ForWord
- Toe By Toe
- All About Learning Press
- Sound Therapy
- Cellfield
- Mind Mapping

Chapter Four   92
Oh, say can you say (if this is related to dyslexia?)
Overlapping specific learning difficulties and health challenges.

- What is the definition of the term 'Learning Difficulty'?
- Overlapping learning challenges
- ADD/ADHD
- Auditory Processing Disorder
- Dyspraxia
- Dysgraphia
- Dyscalculia
- Time
- Other learning challenges
- Health challenges
- The genetics of dyslexia – skin conditions and allergies
- Food intolerances/the gut
- Coeliac disease and gluten sensitivity
- Lactose intolerance

- General dietary changes
- Iron deficiency
- Fatty acid deficiency
- Sugar issues
- Zinc deficiency
- Addictions

Chapter Five   140

How dyslexia stole Christmas (and joy in general)

The social effects of dyslexia.

- Shame
- Embarrassment
- Low self-esteem, anxiety and depression
- The effect on the family of having a child with dyslexia
- An inability to identify and name feelings
- Vulnerability to abuse
- Bullying and cyberbullying
- Self-harm and suicide
- The need for protection from toxic people and unhealthy relationships

Chapter Six   167

My book about me

The importance of finding strengths and competencies.

- Success attributes
- Filling your child's emotional tank
- Debriefing after school
- The role of intuition
- The benefits of a spiritual life

Chapter Seven   183

I can draw, build, design and sing

Nurturing the talents which often come with dyslexia.

- The Arts
- Music
- Visual Arts
- Acting
- Science
- Sport
- Engineering
- Entrepreneurship

Chapter Eight   211

Oh, the lengths you'll go to

A review of the book's ten tips and facts along with the success attributes uncovered by the Frostig Center.

Acknowledgements   219

Bibliography

At the end of the book you will find a link to my website, dyslexiaoctopus.com, where we can continue this conversation.

Enjoy!

Introduction

And to think I saw it on Molesworth Street

In 1981 – the year of Charles and Di's wedding, the invention of Pac-Man and floppy discs – I had my most embarrassing job interview. To be fair, initially it had gone well. I'd managed to come across as a competent fifteen-year-old and the bookstore manager, a young Adolf Hitler look-alike, called Mr Fowler, had offered me the lofty position of Saturday counter assistant. I was elated. He began filling out the required paperwork and then asked a question which almost made my heart stop.

"How do you spell your mother's name?"

I know what you're thinking – what's the big deal? Well, my mother is called Sylvia, but being an English Geordie lass, I'd only ever called her Mam, and because spelling is my nemesis, I had absolutely no idea how to spell her name. My face flushed. I held my breath and dug my nails into the palms of my hands. Then it occurred to me that Mr Fowler didn't know how to spell her name either.

S I L V E A, I enunciated. He looked up and then, as I exhaled, he wrote down exactly what I'd said. I tried to appear interested in his spiel about tax and sick leave, but as he flicked onto the final page, he flummoxed me again.

"What size uniform do you want?"

My mind went blank.

As a bit of background, I wasn't brought up in a nudist colony. Living in the freezing Northeast of England, clothes were a necessity not an optional extra, but at that moment I didn't have a clue of my dress size. "K..k..kind of big," I stammered before fleeing the room, burning with shame.

Little did I realise I'd just been slide tackled by, what I now call, the dyslexia octopus.

At a writing workshop I attended, the tutor, Joe Bennett, described the act of writing as, "Extending a hand to a stranger to offer comfort in the midst of life." I prefer to think of this book as a conversation about dyslexia between two parents at the school gate. In these Covid-19 times, I find it socially awkward offering a hand to a stranger. Whose hand is it? Where's it been?

Time and time again, I find the tidbits of information I pick up when I collect my son from school more useful than anything I learnt toiling away in the classroom. Who knew that sweet potato could be made into tasty biscuits or popping pillowcases in the freezer kills nits? Top tip, remove the pillow first.

I want to share with you some interesting information I've discovered while parenting my dyslexic son. To make this more fun, I'd like to give you, my dear reader, a name; otherwise, I'm talking to myself at this school gate. If you've ever followed me around the supermarket, you'll know I frequently talk to myself, *Milk. Where's the milk? What's next on my list?*

Acronyms can be helpful, TVNZ, BBC, CNN etc. I'm tossing up between:

JACK (Just Aware Curious/ Knowledgeable)

or DIANE (Dyslexia Interested And Needing Explanations).

The politically correct thing to do would be to flick between the two. I'm all for gender equality, but I'll get myself in a muddle. So, for clarity, I'll chat to DIANE. JACK, please feel free to eavesdrop.

I think of dyslexia as a huge octopus wearing a wrestling leotard – the kind of creature made famous by Dr. Seuss. He's my all-time children's book hero. It has taken me years to tackle my own dyslexia octopus. For many years I was determined to hide it at all costs. It had, after all, caused me plenty of embarrassing moments.

I'm sure many people who've met me have wondered if I'm mad or a pathological liar because, when asked a perfectly straightforward question, I sometimes come out with an odd or obviously incorrect answer. In researching this book, I have come to appreciate dyslexia affects much more than spelling, writing and reading. It's a brain wiring difference.

The mental filing cabinet of a dyslexic person doesn't work in the same way as that of a non-dyslexic person.

Don't believe me? Okay, here's an example. Once, when I was visiting my friend in hospital after the birth of her son, I was introduced to her other visitor. We exchanged pleasantries, and she mentioned she was a teacher. My friend said my mother also taught.

"Oh, what age does she teach?" the visitor asked.

"Secondary school," I replied.

Now my mother is, and always has been, a primary school teacher. Why I said secondary is beyond me. Sometimes my brain just fails to find the correct word quickly enough. When I've made such a blooper, I'm torn between explaining my mistake or continuing with the falsehood hoping not to appear an idiot who doesn't know her mother's job.

My mother was a teacher, but I was not assessed for dyslexia. In primary school, I could learn my spelling words before a test, but they slipped away the very next day, like fried eggs off Teflon. I now know that it takes a non-dyslexic child thirty-five sightings of a word to learn it. However, it takes a dyslexic child many, many more sightings to commit a word to long-term memory.

My dyslexia epiphany (thank you spell-checker) happened in Wellington, New Zealand, in 2013. In a swish central city gallery on Molesworth Street, I saw an exhibition entitled *The Secret Art of Dr. Seuss*. During his life, Dr. Seuss (real name Theodor Geisel) painted colourful canvases late at night after he'd finished his day job. According to his wife Audrey, "Painting was what he did for himself and not something he felt comfortable sharing.[1]"

As I wandered around the exhibition, I was bombarded with the images of mazes, intricate patterns, alien worlds and Escher-like optical illusions. I saw a man expressing through art the way I often feel. One image he produced in 1968 profoundly moved me. *Fooling Nobody* is an ink and watercolour drawing of a weird penguin-like bird, walking with an enormous hat on its head. The hat looks like the head of an entirely different creature. It has a nose instead of a beak and is topped with a fancy hairdo. This is the image the bird hopes to project but, as the title suggests, the creature is fooling nobody. Seeing this drawing made me realise that it was time to 'come out' of the dyslexic closet. Maybe I too was fooling nobody.

The main inspiration for baring my soul has been my son Harry, who is also dyslexic. I don't want him to spend his life trying to fool people the way I have done. Unless dyslexics speak up and show that it is okay to be the way we are, society will continue to think of dyslexia as a mental weakness, a fault, something best kept quiet, instead of simply a different way of seeing the world. In the following chapters, I hope to demystify dyslexia using examples from my life, as well as my son's. Just as no two fingerprints are the same, no two dyslexics are identical. Harry and I have different challenges, and yet we share some common traits. By showing some of the lesser-known aspects of dyslexia, I hope to empower people to accept that these are not personal failings. I also want to explain how I have helped my son tackle his own dyslexia octopus and cope at school.

Dyslexia comes with many strengths which are to be celebrated – some call dyslexia their superpower. Dyslexic inventors and entrepreneurs are behind many of the things that have revolutionised our world.

I would prefer to use the term 'person with dyslexia' rather than 'dyslexic' because I appreciate we are all made up of many parts. One label doesn't explain a whole person, but for the purposes of simplicity I have at times used the term dyslexic.

Grab a cuppa DIANE, and settle back, while I uncover some of the less well-known aspects of having dyslexia. I'll tip my hat to Dr. Seuss and his amazing imaginary world by basing my chapter titles on his fabulous books.

Chapter One

The shape of me (and my dyslexia)

Life is Like a Landscape

Having reached my half-century, for the most part bumbling through the landscape of my life with my shoelaces tied together, I can now stop and review my journey.

I feel like I've been given a pair of binoculars with which to look back over my life from the crest of this middle-aged hill.

As Charles Lindbergh once said:

"Life is like a landscape. You live in the midst of it but can describe it only from the vantage point of distance." (Flight's Enigmatic Hero)

The thought of writing this book terrified me. I write for a living but have started and stopped this project numerous times. DIANE, I appreciate that you are busy. There are dishes in the sink, the car needs a service, bills must be paid; you need to get something out of chatting at this metaphorical school gate. There's a lot of technical information about teaching dyslexics that makes me want to rip out my eyeballs. I'll leave that to other books. I'll suggest useful web links instead. I'm a storyteller and a visual learner; I've never read my TV instruction booklet. If this sounds like you, I think you'll appreciate my approach.

Paula's Story

In 2002 I met Paula. She was in her mid-forties, severely overweight, and because she had arthritis, she wore splints on both wrists and required a stick to walk any distance. She had a husband and two children, and her family was struggling. I tried to get alongside her. What I soon discovered was a web of issues which would make any arachnophobe run for the hills. Suffering from severe anxiety and depression made it difficult for her to organise and run her home. As a couple, they were under terrible financial pressure and their house was in danger of being repossessed. She confided in me that she been sexually abused as a child but had never had any counselling around the attack. Paula was addicted to Coca-Cola and drank two litres per day. She continually craved sweet foods.

Hayden, her thirteen-year-old son, was severely bullied both at school and by the children in their neighbourhood. Paula knew Hayden had learning difficulties, but his school hadn't identified them, nor were they offering him any learning support. Paula's financial problems meant she could not afford the $700 to have her son privately assessed. Whenever Hayden came to my house, he tripped up or knocked things over. I now appreciate he was severely dyspraxic as well as dyslexic. After attempting suicide at the age of sixteen, he finally got the attention of the mental health professionals, who put some support in place for him, but not before he'd dropped out of school and become involved in the Drugs' scene.

Paula had no qualifications. She had never been diagnosed as dyslexic, but she struggled with spelling, and her handwriting looked like that of a six-year-old. During the three years I was her friend, we became close. She was profoundly spiritual and enjoyed attending a Christian church. Her other pleasure in life was reading Charles

Dickens. She was a member of the Dickens Society and loved being able to lose herself in his stories. Although at the time I empathised with Paula, I didn't appreciate just how similar we were. Over the years I have been drawn to help people like Paula, misguidedly thinking it was my compassionate nature (dyslexics score highly on empathy, which is why we make great health care professionals and social workers). I now appreciate I could so easily have found myself in Paula's shoes had my dyslexia been more severe, and had I not had such lucky breaks.

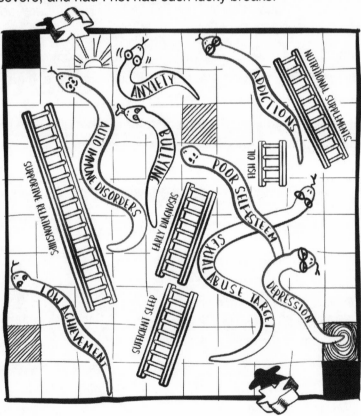

As I write this, I can hear a dog barking outside in the street, and I have to smile. My picture-thinking brain has made the connection between my thoughts on Paula's situation and the barking dog. I guess to some people this idea of health and social issues being connected to dyslexia will seem barking mad. I have, however, experienced this in my life and have seen it in other people. What is more, it has been confirmed by research. Sadly, by middle-age, many people who have dyslexia suffer from similar problems. Unpicking Paula's story reveals a number of challenges which I will address in the following chapters.

As a parent, being forearmed is extremely helpful. The issues your child is facing may be typical for a child with dyslexia. I will give you tips on what has helped my son and discuss some useful resources, which I hope will help you avoid ending up in Paula's or Hayden's situation.

According to a UK report, the percentage of dyslexic prison inmates may be as high as 57%.

I don't wish to scare you, but if a dyslexic child is not able to overcome their difficulties, their outcome may be grim. I'm not saying this is inevitable; I have never darkened the doors of a prison, but in 2008 a New Zealand Ministry of Education report showed that 90% of prison inmates were functionally illiterate, and 80% were not functionally numerate.[2] It is estimated that 10-15% of New Zealand's population have dyslexia and yet, according to a UK report,[3] the percentage of dyslexic inmates may be as high as 57%.

"There are currently few studies exploring prevalence rates of different specific learning difficulties in young offenders. However, specific reading difficulties, such as dyslexia, appear significantly more common in young people who offend, with research studies suggesting a prevalence of between 43 and 57%, compared to around 10% of the general population.[3]"

Heartbreaking, I'm sure you'll agree, and a spur to ensure, as parents, we do all we can to keep our children from joining these statistics.

Chapter Two

Bunches of hunches. Does my child have dyslexia?

Welcoming Harry into our Family

I am a collector. No, I didn't say a hoarder – I'm not confessing any OCD tendencies here (hmm, a topic for another book, methinks). I have a magpie's eye for a pretty leaf or shiny stone. There's a green pebble the size of a quail's egg next to my computer. It has ripples of white and beige running through it and, when wet, it looks like jade. It blows my mind that these strata were laid down millions of years ago and were caused by tremendous geological pressures. To some, such a pebble appears flawed, but to me, it is the layers that add interest and make it beautiful. A plain green stone wouldn't be such a treasure.

In 2005, my husband and I were fortunate to adopt a twelve-day-old baby boy. We named him Harry. He came into the world not as a small pebble, but as a rolling boulder; 11lbs 12oz at birth (over 5 kilos): the size of an average three-month-old!

We had been blessed with a daughter in 2002, and we thought that we had the parenting thing sorted. I believe that we were sent Harry to knock off our parenting-pride edges. We went from having SPF 50 to SPF 0 in the space of a few days. (SPF here denotes Smug Parent Factor, not sunscreen.) From day one, nothing about Harry was like his sister. We now understand that he struggles with dyslexia and attention deficit disorder (ADD). We were utterly flummoxed.

SPF 50

SPF 0

As a baby and toddler, his ADD was the primary challenge for us. It was only when he went to school that we began to suspect he also had dyslexia. It may surprise you I didn't recognise his dyslexia, but I was undiagnosed at that stage. It's only in parenting Harry that I have researched dyslexia and come to appreciate many of my own quirks and struggles are in fact part of the condition.

What is Dyslexia?

In 2009, a UK government report provided the following definition of dyslexia[4]:

> "Dyslexia is a learning difficulty that primarily affects the skills involved in accurate and fluent word reading and spelling. Characteristic features of dyslexia are difficulties in phonological awareness, verbal memory and verbal processing speed. Dyslexia occurs across the range of intellectual abilities. It is best thought of as a continuum, not a distinct category, and there are no clear cut-off points. Co-occurring difficulties may be seen in aspects of language, motor co-ordination, mental calculation, concentration and personal organisation, but these are not, by themselves, markers of dyslexia. A good indication of the severity and persistence of dyslexic difficulties can be gained by examining how the individual responds or has responded to well-founded intervention."

As a parent of a dyslexic child, it's easy to beat yourself up and think that your child's difficulties are in some way your fault. Everything else seems to be your fault, right? Rest assured, dyslexia is not caused by your divorce, TV viewing habits, inconsistent boundaries or busy family life.

"Dyslexia is neurobiological in origin, meaning that the problem is located physically in the brain. Dyslexia is not caused by poverty, developmental delay, speech or hearing impairments, or learning a second language, although those conditions may put a child more at risk for developing a reading disability.[5]"

It has been estimated that up to 17% of children have dyslexia,[6] yet a UK government report has suggested that 80% of them are not diagnosed,[7] while in the US it has been suggested only five out of every 100 dyslexics are recognised and receive assistance.[8] Sorry, but I feel the need to stand on my chair and yell – 95% of students don't get any help!

only 5 out of every 100 dyslexics are recognised and receive assistance

The consequence of this is that millions of people struggle through life oblivious to the fact that they are wrestling with the dyslexia octopus. Also, in the past, teachers couldn't identify students with dyslexia. This has led to parents and grandparents finally understanding their own learning difficulties when their children or grandchildren receive a diagnosis.

Dyslexia occurs on a continuum: one family member may have a little trouble with spelling, but another may be unable to read even a one-syllable word such as 'cat'. Because dyslexia looks different for each person, it can be difficult to spot the links. I'm not sure who else in my family is dyslexic; in fact, they were shocked when I said I was. They thought, as I used to, I was just hopeless at spelling. Because dyslexia is an inherited condition, if one parent has dyslexia, their child has a 40–60% chance of inheriting it.[9] It can skip generations. It will be found in all the rings if you cut a cross-section through your family tree, but please don't try this at home – I don't want to be responsible for your family keeling over. It's only because children in the last 150 years have had to sit quietly in rows at school and learn to read and write that dyslexia has become more apparent.

Dean Bragonier is the Founder, and Executive Dyslexic of NoticeAbility, an organisation aimed at helping children with dyslexia recognise their strengths. In his 2015 TEDx talk, he stated:[10]

"In the first nine-tenths of human existence, societies were largely based on apprentice models, from hunter and gatherers, down to the trades in more recent times, people learned by observing and then doing kinesthetic learning. Now, this happens to be the wheelhouse for dyslexics, this is our prime opportunity to learn."

He goes on to say that the Industrial Revolution changed education and this, coupled with the invention of the printing press, "essentially locked the door on 20% of the population".

For more on Dean Bragonier, check out his pioneering school for dyslexics at www.noticeability.org.

The Dyslexia Octopus

As mentioned previously, DIANE, I see dyslexia as an octopus. This is because it creates challenges in eight different areas:

- Spatial and temporal abilities
- Motor control problems
- Reading difficulties
- Listening difficulties
- Spelling issues
- Writing difficulties
- Memory difficulties
- Social and health issues

Potential Areas of Difficulty For Someone With Dyslexia

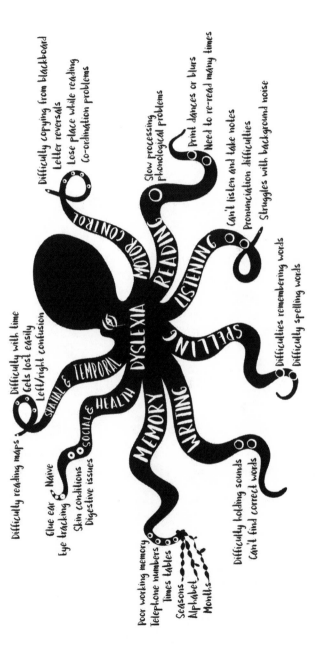

On the previous page is a mind map of the sort of difficulties a dyslexic person may encounter. Please bear in mind that a person doesn't have to have all these challenges to be diagnosed with dyslexia. For example, these days I don't have motor control problems (although I did reverse Ds and Bs as a child), but I can relate to many of the other expressions of dyslexia to some degree.

Signs of Dyslexia in Young Children

If you are wondering about whether your child has dyslexia, here are some common early indications.

A child with dyslexia may:

- Learn to talk later than other children. Some do not start speaking until as late as three or four.
- Lisp, stutter or have some other speech impediment.
- Have a squint.
- Have frequent ear infections in the early years.
- Have difficulty learning the names of shapes or colours.
- Have difficulty identifying letter names and sounds.
- Reverse syllables and phonemes (letter sounds) within a word.
- Struggle to sequence days of the week, months of the year, the alphabet, and numbers.
- Have trouble recognising written letters in words or even in their name.

- Be delayed with fine motor skills like tying shoelaces, colouring and writing.
- Have trouble with telling the time and understanding the concept of time, for example, mixing up breakfast, lunch and dinner.
- Struggle to learn to ride a bike.
- Take longer to learn to swim.

Please do refer to this list if your child is taking longer than other children to master something new. I spent a small fortune on swimming lessons for Harry, and even paid for private lessons before I realised he just wasn't ready to learn. We went back to lessons a few years later and he became a great swimmer, going on to become his school's champion and compete in swimming competitions. His early swimming lessons did nothing for his constant ear infections, which happened with every tooth he cut (more about this in my chapter on health).

Rest assured dyslexia is not caused by your divorce, TV viewing habits, inconsistent boundaries or busy family life.

Teaching Harry to ride a bike was also a completely different experience to teaching his sister. With her, we'd put trainer wheels on her bicycle and allowed her to get used to cycling. After a couple of months, we went to a wide beach, which had a stretch of compacted sand, and took off the trainer wheels. We spent a couple of hours running up and down the beach holding on to her bike as she rode, then letting go. She had a few tumbles but mastered the balancing and was off and away. We did the same thing for Harry. We got nowhere. The trainer wheels stayed on the bike for another year. Then, one day at a friend's house, Harry spotted a bike on the lawn. He hopped on and cycled down the street. My jaw hit the ground. I began to appreciate Harry does everything in his own sweet time!

Types of Dyslexia

Dyslexia isn't like diabetes; there isn't Type 1 and Type 2. In fact, no one has produced an official list of variations. That's mainly because most people with dyslexia have more than one form. Dyslexia can be the result of a head injury, but in this book, I'm talking about the type a person is born with, developmental dyslexia. These are the five subtypes of this form of dyslexia:

Phonological Dyslexia – difficulty in breaking down individual sounds of language and connecting sounds to written symbols.

Surface Dyslexia – problems seeing and remembering whole words.

Rapid Naming Deficit – difficulty in rapidly naming letters. This is connected to processing speed and reading speed.

Double Deficit Dyslexia – weak phonological awareness

as well as rapid naming deficit.

Visual Dyslexia – unusual visual disturbances when reading, such as letters switching places on the page.

The fact that there are so many variants explains why an intervention which works well for one person may not help someone else, even if they are siblings.

For more information see:

The understood.org page on types of dyslexia https:// archive.vn/PDuJn archived webpage.
The Reading Well https://archive.ph/Gwcv7 archived webpage.

Differences in the Dyslexic Brain

Researchers have been able to see the differences in brains in recent years with SPECT brain imaging, and by studying the brains of dead dyslexics (sounds rather messy). Gordon Sherman, a dyslexia expert, writes,[11]

"While no two brains are alike, the brains of people with dyslexia are distinctly different compared to those without dyslexia. Dyslexic brains function differently because they are organized differently. They even look different, though not to the naked eye. Scientists use microscopes and sophisticated neuroimaging tools to study the structural and functional differences of dyslexic brains."

Sherman goes on to say that dyslexic brains are more symmetrical and that, "they have smaller neurons in certain cell clusters (nuclei) of the thalamus. The two affected nuclei are dedicated to vision and hearing."

In a nutshell, the brain of a dyslexic person has smaller cells in the areas which control seeing and hearing. This may seem disheartening news, but Sherman points out that many dyslexics have exceptional strengths and "given the fact that environments always change, who knows what diverse minds our species will need in the future?"

How cool would it be if being dyslexic turned out to be essential for the survival of the species?

Check out Dean Bragonier's TEDx talk entitled 'The True Gifts of a Dyslexic Mind,' for more about brain differences.

www.youtube.com/watch?v=_dPyzFFcG7A

Left Brain and Right Brain Tasks

According to Dyslexia Victoria Online:[12]

"The 'big picture' is dyslexics are dominant right brain learners and thinkers in a society that reflects and respects the thinking processes of the left brain. 'Righties' can have a difficult time fitting in... This is not to say that being a left-brain thinker is better. They have their weaknesses and limitations with certain types of processing also."

Dyslexics are right-brained thinkers. Here is a list of the kind of things each side of the brain is good at:

Left Brain Tasks
- Analytical thinking – breaking complex problems into their component parts
- Language
- Science
- Logic
- Maths

Right Brain Tasks
- Holistic thinking – seeing the bigger picture rather than separate parts
- Creativity
- Intuition
- Music
- Art

That explains a lot for me as I'm creative, arty and very intuitive. Harry is musical, creative and intuitive.

Did I hear you ask if I would swap my brain for a non-dyslexic version? Well, it would be rather nice to have two heads – I would switch between my dyslexic and non-dyslexic head, depending on the task. The problem is, such an approach to life would call for an entirely new wardrobe. All my tops would require an extra opening – far too expensive.

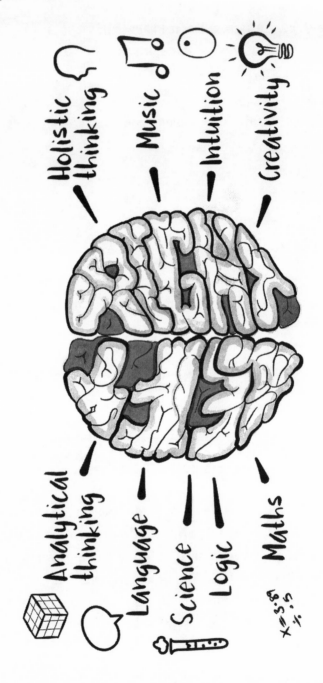

Why Get an Assessment for Dyslexia?

For some, hearing that their child has dyslexia is upsetting. However, I believe everyone is on some continuum or other. This isn't about being picked out as being weird or different; it's about understanding how your child's brain is wired.

About ten years ago, I volunteered at a youth group for children with severe physical disabilities. Most of the kids in the group were non-verbal and depended on their carers, yet their individuality shone through. Some could tell jokes using keypads; others enjoyed shaking instruments along to the music we played. One of the other volunteers was a teenage girl. I remember her saying to the leader, "I'm so glad that I'm not like these kids. They can't do anything." To which the leader gently answered, "We're all like these kids. We all have strengths and weaknesses. The only difference is their weaknesses are obvious."

I've come to realise that labelling people as 'normal' or 'abnormal' is unhelpful. Everyone just makes the best of whatever hand life deals them.

Speaking of hands, I love Hans Christian Andersen's story, *The Ugly Duckling*. Andersen may or may not have had dyslexia, but he described his school days as "the bitterest time of my life". In his story, the ugly duckling compares himself to others and feels ashamed and embarrassed by his differences. It is only when he realises that he is a swan, not a duck, that he can blossom.

Getting a dyslexia diagnosis is the first step to lifting the mantle of shame. My friends' children are a case in point. It is obvious to me that they are somewhere on the dyslexia spectrum. However, I find my friends aren't prepared to discuss the subject. They claim it would be harmful to label their children. My response is whether they like it or not, their kids *will* be labelled. If the label isn't 'dyslexic', it will be 'weird', 'stupid' or 'lazy'. Even if others don't verbalise a label, the child will label themselves. At a time when their self-concept is being cast in concrete, it's heartbreaking to hear a child saying, "I'm so useless and stupid. Everybody else can do such and such at school, except me."

Research has proven that early intervention, while language areas in the brain are still developing, is the most successful way to reduce the long-term impacts of dyslexia.[13]

I have a single-mum friend who struggled to get her child assessed under the public system in New Zealand. Help was only forthcoming once her eight-year-old son started self-harming.

Getting a diagnosis brings mixed feelings but can be empowering. There is the sense of the world suddenly coming into focus for the dyslexic child as they breathe a sigh of relief and say, "So that's why I'm like this!"

When it dawned on me that I had dyslexia, I went through a

range of emotions: embarrassment, shock, disappointment. Then, when I checked out the long list of famous people who are also dyslexic, I felt quite excited – maybe I too have a hidden talent (I'm still looking, it's well hidden).

Famous People with Dyslexia (see Chapter Seven for more).

- Professor Elizabeth Blackburn – Nobel Prize in Medicine
- Richard Branson – Entrepreneur
- Erin Brockovich – Environmental Activist
- Lewis Carroll – Author
- Agatha Christie – Author
- Michael Faraday – Scientist
- Henry Ford – Car Manufacturer
- Whoopi Goldberg – Actor
- Alexander Graham Bell – Inventor
- Carol W. Greider – Molecular Biologist and Nobel Prize winner
- Steve Jobs – Co-founder of Apple Inc.
- Pablo Picasso – Artist
- Guy Ritchie – Film Director
- Jules Verne – Author
- Henry Winkler – Actor

In England in 2017, Made by Dyslexia, a global charity whose aim is to help people understand dyslexia using innovative means, created a fake Dyslexic Sperm Bank to

Henry Ford
Car manufacturer

Alexander Graham Bell
Inventor

Henry Winkler
Actor

Richard Branson
Entrepreneur

Erin Brockovich
Environmental activist

Pierre Curie
Scientist

Lewis Carroll
Author

Elizabeth Blackburn
Nobel Prize in medicine

Pablo Picasso
Artist

Jules Verne
Author

Carol W. Greider
Molecular biologist
and Nobel Prize winner

Whoopi Goldberg
Actor

highlight the need for people to change their perception of the condition. They posted their experiment on YouTube. The two-minute clip is well worth viewing and can be found at: www.youtube.com/watch?v=G7ZaQf-woHg&t=21s

Members of the public were stopped in the street and asked if they would want their child to have dyslexia. No one says yes. Watching this, I felt a wee stab to my heart. The same people were then shown a catalogue of potential sperm donors, all of whom have or had dyslexia. The 'donors' all excelled in their fields, including John Lennon, Henry Ford, Alexander Graham Bell, and Steve Jobs. When confronted with this fact, the people expressed amazement at the contribution people with dyslexia have made to the world.

At What Age Should I Get My Child Assessed?

Harry exhibited signs of dyslexia from when he was first introduced to letters. He didn't pick up the alphabet, couldn't write his name, and when he did write letters, they were usually reversed. At his primary school, I felt teachers viewed me as a 'pushy mother' whenever I queried his lack of progress. They repeatedly assured me there was nothing to worry about. If we had accepted their assessment, he might have gone right through primary school without getting help. Please don't think I am knocking any particular school. Teachers are busy with large classes and must plan their lessons for a wide range of ability. There are few teaching assistants, and the ones available need to help the children with more severe learning difficulties. Budget cuts mean there is no incentive for schools to identify children who may have dyslexia because getting a diagnosis sets the family up to be frustrated when no state help is forthcoming. When Harry was a few weeks away from his seventh birthday, we paid to have him privately tested for dyslexia.

That day is burned into my brain.

At that time, Harry's ADD wasn't under control. Sitting for hours of testing was torturous for him. When we got the results back, his IQ was deemed high, as were his verbal comprehension index and perceptual reasoning. The difficulties lay with his working memory and processing speed. The report highlighted issues with his speech and sequencing ability. He had a very small bank of sight words and struggled to recognise high-frequency words. Following instructions was a challenge for him, as was maintaining a steady level of attention, grasping the concept of time and quantity, and putting ideas down onto paper. Despite having all the indications, he wasn't diagnosed as dyslexic because the test administrator told me it wasn't possible to diagnose dyslexia before the age of seven.

I was furious.

She knew his age at the outset, but hadn't thought to mention the age restriction for diagnosis *before* I handed over my cash.

Throughout the world, research is being conducted which indicates it is possible to identify dyslexia in preschool children. Prof. Gail Gillon at the University of Canterbury has developed an online assessment tool which tests for phonological awareness. Phonology is the study of the distribution and patterning of speech sounds in a language.[14] It is thought that if children at preschool level who are having difficulty with phonological awareness can be identified and offered additional support, their literacy problems with dyslexia may be reduced. Some people argue there are several reasons why a child may be slow to read and write; dyslexia is only one. Therefore, it is best not to test before seven. However, if you are aware of a family history of dyslexia, I would urge you to be proactive in seeking a diagnosis as early as possible.

Early intervention, while language areas in the brain are still developing is the most successful way to reduce the long-term impacts of dyslexia.

The National Institutes of Health (NIH) research project in the early 1980s, which tracked 5,000 children, starting when they were four years old until they graduated from high school, found that dyslexia could be identified with 92% accuracy at ages 5 ½ to 6 ½.[15] The researchers tested these children three times a year for fourteen years using a variety of tests, but they did not provide any intervention. From that research, they were able to determine which tests identify reading failure and at what age it can be picked up. They also proved that children do not outgrow reading failure or dyslexia, and to improve they require explicit instruction on phonemic awareness.

If your child is showing signs of dyslexia at primary school, I suggest asking the teacher to find out what your education service can provide. If nothing is forthcoming, find out who is qualified to make a dyslexia diagnosis in your area. If you are in New Zealand, there is talk of free dyslexia screening for all primary school children being rolled out in the next few years. I hope this happens. In the meantime, if you can afford it, you may have to pay to have your child assessed. When you find someone who offers dyslexia assessment, double-check that they are qualified. Ask what is involved in the testing and what kind of report they will produce. And please learn from my mistake – make sure they consider your child old enough to make a diagnosis of dyslexia.

If your child is at secondary school, they may require an assessment to access a reader/writer or extra time with examinations. In New Zealand this assessment must be no more than three years old. I waited until Harry was almost fifteen to have his next full assessment done. This was because I wanted it to last until he finished school. I know some schools will arrange this extra support without requiring an independent assessment, so talk to the Head of Learning Support at your child's school before booking one.

Chapter Three

Harry Hears a Who, but has no idea it starts

with the letter 'W'

My Learning Challenges

I grew up in the Northeast of England, in a lower-middle-class home (social class is a fundamental part of life in England). Apparently, as a child, I was a dreamer and often misheard things or didn't understand what people said. I remember, aged six, my mother saying she was going to do some ironing. I asked her where the mine was. She thought I was cheeky. I wasn't; I just struggled to hear the subtleties in speech.

Primary school was confusing. My first classroom had an alphabet frieze running around the top of the walls. This image is burned into my brain; I spent so much time studying it. Try as I may, I couldn't remember the sequence of letters, L M N…???

In the 1970s, few teachers had heard of, or understood dyslexia (sadly, in many schools, not much has changed). Back then, teachers said children who struggled to learn were lazy or stupid. Surely, an intelligent child who has been taught to spell February yesterday, couldn't forget that word by the next day. This happened to me when I was nine years old. My teacher, Mr West, who was a well-meaning chap, had a rule that if the date was misspelt, it had to be written out 100 times per day of the month. I misspelt it on February the 28th and therefore had to write it out 2,800 times at home, which I obediently did (what were my parents thinking?). The crazy thing is I still struggle to spell February and don't get me started on Wednesday.

In *Hold on to Your Kids*, child psychologist, Gordon Neufeld and author Gabor Maté write: "Children learn best when they like their teacher, and they think their teacher likes them.[16]" It is, therefore, no surprise that many dyslexic children struggle to learn at school if they feel judged and shamed.

As mentioned earlier, brain scans have proved dyslexics have very different brain patterns to non-dyslexics, and this affects their ability to remember spelling words. These kids are not mucking about – yes, I am looking at you, Mr West. Bitter? Me?

When I reached high school, I excelled in English, but

my spelling was atrocious. My teacher pulled me out of class one morning and sat me down to learn a list of ten words. She immediately tested me and, because I got them all right, she told me I didn't have dyslexia; I was just hopeless at spelling. Had she tested me on the same words the following week, I wouldn't have got many correct. She knew very little about dyslexia. This test did wonders for my confidence – NOT! I had very successful older siblings, and I was determined not to be the family failure. From then on, I worked ridiculously hard and copied from friends when necessary to get me through school.

"Children learn best when they like their teacher, and they think their teacher likes them."

Gordon Neufeld

Foreign languages were particularly problematic. Having seen the illustration of brain hemispheres, I now understand why. I loved the sound of French and would often sit up late at night listening to French radio programmes. Despite my tremendous efforts, I found learning verb conjugations difficult. I've since been told that Spanish and Japanese are good second languages for English speakers who have dyslexia. Unfortunately, these were not an option for me. At sixteen, I sat Latin, French and German 'O' levels, and was disappointed when I only scraped a pass in each. What was I thinking? I could hardly spell in English, no wonder I struggled to write foreign languages.

I will not let Harry make the same mistake. I have suggested he does other options and skips foreign languages altogether. He may be able to pick one up later, but for now, I'm not going to burden him with yet more spelling words.

Key Early Years' Issues

The following section documents some of the issues Harry had in his early years. That's not to say everyone who has dyslexia will struggle with all these issues, but I wish I'd known back then these problems may be related to dyslexia. It would have saved me time and money. I hope you find this helpful.

I'm a mum at the school gate, DIANE, not a doctor. I'll talk more about health later in the book, but do consult a medical professional if you are concerned about your child's health.

1. The Impact of Ear Infections

Do you remember I mentioned speech difficulties might be an early sign of dyslexia? Harry didn't start speaking until he was well over two years old. At that stage, all he could say was Mam, (my northern dialect sounded super cute coming out of the mouth of a little Kiwi), bye-bye, okay and poo. Some would argue what more does a boy need to say. However, I was concerned about his lack of vocabulary.

The health professionals I consulted, told me that boys often talk later than girls and that a second child can be lazy because the oldest child talks for them. Something I have come to appreciate is that a mother's instinct is usually correct. No one knows your child like you do.

From the time he began teething at four months, Harry had multiple ear infections. He had seven teeth by the age of one, and with every new tooth, the doctor gave him a course of antibiotics. I look back and cringe. I believe all those antibiotics devastated his gut and exacerbated the health issues I'll discuss later. He should have been prescribed probiotics to help repopulate his gut. He also spent months with sore ears. Possibly this affected his hearing and his ability to pick up language.

There is a link between suffering from glue ear (this is called otitis media), requiring grommets, and having dyslexia.[17] This is a complex subject and requires a book in its own right. Certainly, not all children who need grommets have dyslexia, but the two conditions often look very similar.

The reason infants get more ear infections than adults is that their Eustachian tubes are so small. In 80% of children, the fluid usually clears up within twelve weeks, but when liquid is in the middle ear for more than two weeks, it is called glue ear (otitis media). The eardrum cannot vibrate and carry noise vibrations to the inner ear when there is fluid present. Here's some guff about this tricky little tube.

"The Eustachian tube of an adult sits at a 45° angle, while the angle is approximately 10° in infants. Additionally, an infant's Eustachian tube measures approximately 18 mm in length; the tube grows rapidly during childhood, reaching its adult length of 3–4 cm by age 7 years.[18]"

The ear

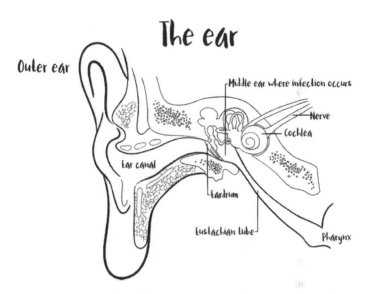

Outer ear

Middle ear where infection occurs

Nerve

Cochlea

Ear canal

Eardrum

Eustachian tube

Pharynx

With my son, the treatment recommended by our family doctor was numerous courses of antibiotics. I do hope a different approach is being taken today for repeat ear infections. The insertion of small tubes, called grommets, through the eardrum to release pressure and drain fluid is a standard treatment for glue ear. These grommets drop out after about six months, and new ones may be required if the problem persists.

Harry did not get grommets, but I have no doubt his

multiple ear infections caused fluid to build up in his ears. I once read that people with dyslexia have shorter and narrower Eustachian tubes, which may explain why they are susceptible to ear infections.

Equalising pressure in the ears when flying has always been difficult for me. Now I appreciate this is connected to my ear structure.

One option for repeat ear infections is non-surgical products such as *Otovent* or *EarPopper*. These weren't around when Harry was a baby, and therefore I'm not able to comment on their effectiveness.

Key Overlaps Between Dyslexia and Glue Ear

- The slow speed of processing spoken and/or written language
- Poor concentration
- Difficulty following instructions
- Forgetting words
- Bizarre spelling: not age/ability appropriate
- Difficulty in blending letters together
- Difficulty in establishing syllable division or knowing the beginning or endings of words
- Unusual pronunciation of words
- Poor comprehension. Laboured when reading, especially out loud

- Difficulty in picking up the key points from a passage
- Limited understanding of non-verbal communication
- Prone to daydream
- Easily distracted. Is the class clown, disruptive or withdrawn
- Excessively tired due to the amount of concentration and effort required for schoolwork.[19]

Dr Lindsay Peer is a dyslexia expert, and a fellow of the International Academy for Research in Learning Disabilities. She has examined the link between glue ear, multilingualism and dyslexia (interestingly she states there are higher rates of dyslexia amongst multilingual students) and found that there was a significantly higher incidence of ear infections in people with dyslexia. In dyslexic multilingual children, 70% had suffered from severe glue ear.[19] She postulates that there may be a genetic predisposition in dyslexic children to glue ear. Check out her fascinating talk on YouTube http://www.youtube.com/watch?v=lTqzisNRxPA. Your GP may be dismissive of any link between dyslexia and glue ear, and you may wish to show them this too.

Resolving glue ear is essential for a child to succeed in school. Grommet surgery may be necessary. If publicly funded treatment has a long waiting list, if funds allow, you may decide to access private health care to speed up the process. Months of hearing loss at an early age can lead to delays in speech and learning.

A mother whose son required grommets but did not have dyslexia told me that missing out on hearing for an extended period during the early years can cause delays even once the child can hear. The brain must go through the set stages of language development required for fluent speech. These won't happen overnight following surgery.

Issues due to ear problems can look like dyslexia and may be worsened by the fact that many boys are not ready for school at the age of five. Perhaps this is one reason dyslexia testing is not recommended in New Zealand before the age of seven? By this age, children who were educationally delayed due to ear problems have usually caught up.

While researching glue ear, I found a paper saying some ethnic groups have higher rates of otitis media. In New Zealand, Maori and Pacific children have the highest rates, because of the physiological structure of the ear canal – predominately smaller tubes. This may be a factor in their lower levels of educational achievement.[20]

Another issue for children with reduced hearing is that noisy environments make it difficult to hear the teacher. This is particularly relevant to open-plan teaching environments. A child who is effectively locked out of learning by not being able to catch instructions will often act out their frustration and exhibit behavioural problems.

Top Fact 1

There is a link between dyslexia and glue ear.

Top Tip 1

Check with your doctor to rule out glue ear if your child

has the issues listed in this section.

---

2. The Impact of Speech Difficulties

Harry had a speech impediment until he was almost seven years old. Other people thought we were lazy in not constantly correcting his speech, but we knew he felt judged whenever we did. Rather than point out every word he said incorrectly, we repeated what he had said and inserted the correct word. For example, when he said, "Where's Yelly", we would say, "Kelly is over there." Or he'd say, "too too train", and we'd say, "Yes, it is a choo choo train."

"A phonogram is a letter or set of two to four letters representing a single voiced sound within a word... Seventy-two phonograms have been identified by Anna Gillingham." [21]

At three and a half, Harry still struggled with the letter blends sh, ch, th, as well as the individual letters F, G, S, V and B.

I took Harry to see a District Health Board speech therapist when he was four, but she assured me his speech was perfectly normal. When he was seven, I found a speech therapist who also taught dyslexic children. She understood Harry's phonological issue and mentioned he probably also had auditory processing disorder. At the time I didn't know much about this (I will touch on it in Chapter Four). She explained Harry couldn't hear the middle sounds in many words. This made perfect sense to me. I found it perplexing we could spell out C, A, T to him, but when we asked what word these letters made, he would say "book" or some other completely unrelated word.

The Shaywitzes, a couple who have spent over thirty years studying dyslexia at the Yale Center for Dyslexia & Creativity, and have followed 445 dyslexic five-year-olds through to adulthood, put it like this:

"People with dyslexia have trouble separating words into phonemes, the sounds that correspond with each part of a word. For example, the word "dog" is broken down into the phonemes "duh," "aah" and "guh".

Hearing these discrete sounds is a vital part of learning to read. But people with dyslexia hear the word only in its entirety: "dog".[22]

Harry's excellent speech therapist spent thirty minutes twice a week for three months getting him to do activities including hopping on letter cards placed around the floor. She trained his ear by getting him to move and say the letter sounds at the same time. I didn't sit in on the lessons, so no doubt there was more to the programme than that, but by the end, he could hear the individual letter sounds. Not surprisingly, it was impossible for him to learn to read or write before he overcame this difficulty.

Phonogram vs Phoneme

A phonogram is a visual symbol used to represent

a speech sound in writing: t, m, oi, ch, igh.

They may contain one letter or more than one.

A phoneme is a distinct, single sound that is used

in the speech of a particular language.

Phonemes are the smallest units of spoken language

and are combined to make words.

The spoken word "cheek" has three phonemes,

which you can hear clearly if you say it aloud

and separate it into its sounds: /ch - ee - k/.

The sounds, not the symbols that represent them,

are the phonemes.

And this spoken word is written with three phonograms:

ch, ee, and k.[23]

Help to overcome phonological weaknesses is available thanks to technology and, if you can afford it, specialist tutoring.

"You need to develop phonic awareness, the ability to break down words into their component sounds – symbolized by the letters of the alphabet. Sally Shaywitz, one of the pioneers in dyslexia studies (and author of 'Overcoming Learning Disabilities'), calls this 'breaking the code.' Fluency is a problem for a dyslexic. Ask an adult to read something aloud. If he stumbles and stops and starts, most likely he has dyslexia. The good news is that he can be treated, no matter what his age.[24]"

Top Fact 2

Speech problems are common for children

with dyslexia.

Top Tip 2

If your child is showing signs of dyslexia, and their speech is unclear, look for a speech therapist who understands dyslexia. The starting point is getting a standard hearing test. Be aware that a child may have excellent hearing but may still have phonological challenges, such as auditory processing disorder, which requires specialist help.

3. The Role of Eye Tracking Difficulties and Irlen Syndrome

Harry had tremendous problems learning to read and write. The physiological aspects hampering him were numerous – there isn't one area of the brain responsible for reading. In evolutionary terms, reading is a recently acquired skill, which requires many parts of the brain to work together.

Harry's school failed to pick up his issues. We live in New Zealand, and dyslexia wasn't officially recognised by our Government until the year 2007. Consequently, many teachers have had little training in how to identify or teach children who have dyslexia.

Before Harry started school, we did the same things with him as we had done with our daughter who'd had no problems learning to read.

- We had stick-on letters in the bath, and every bath-time we made little words.
- We read to him at least once every day.
- We made flashcards with the word for familiar objects such as 'cat' and 'ball'.
- We made books using photographs of him and wrote stories from his daily life.
- We showed him how to write his name (I'm so pleased that we didn't call him Christopher or Stephen, Harry was tricky enough).

When Harry tried to write his name, the letters were usually reversed or, in one memorable incident on the beach, he wrote his name two metres high in the sand – backwards.

After a year's schooling, Harry had made no progress in reading and was put on a programme called Reading Recovery. I'm sure that for some children this works, and I would also like to say that his teacher meant well, however, for a dyslexic child Reading Recovery is like trying to teach a totally deaf child by SHOUTING LOUDER. All the programme did was reinforce a feeling of failure; Harry's self-confidence plummeted, and he began to hate school.

We had Harry's vision tested on a couple of occasions and were assured by the optometrists that there was nothing wrong with his sight; it was better than average. When he was seven, we had him checked for Irlen Syndrome.

What is Irlen Syndrome?

"Irlen Syndrome is a light sensitivity where individuals are sensitive to a specific wavelength of light, and this sensitivity is what causes the physical and visual symptoms ... people with Irlen Syndrome have difficulty reading not because their brains have difficulty connecting the letters they see with the sounds those letters make, but because they see distortions on the printed page, or because the white background or glare hurts their eyes, gives them a headache, or makes them fall asleep while trying to read.

Unlike dyslexia, difficulties experienced as a result of Irlen Syndrome can reach well beyond just reading and writing. People with Irlen Syndrome have difficulties processing all visual information, not just words on a printed page, so they often experience difficulties with depth perception, driving, sports performance and other areas not generally connected with dyslexia. It is possible to suffer from both dyslexia and Irlen Syndrome.[25]"

For people with Irlen Syndrome, using coloured overlays or coloured glasses may help. We tried a couple of different colours. Harry had a blue piece of film, which matched his eyes, and a red one, which matched the overdraft we were clocking up on specialist interventions. For him, neither made any difference. We also spent a memorable summer holiday making him do daily eye tracking exercises. These were the equivalent of forcing your child to walk across scalding coals for twenty minutes a day. My memory of that summer is forever clouded by the crying and tantrums those exercises elicited (that was just from me).

When he was eight years old, I heard at the school gate of an optometrist (the only one in New Zealand) who was offering a *Schoolvision* spectacle prescription, which gives a dyslexic child a lead eye (one eye leads the way when reading). The optometrist claimed that often people with dyslexia who struggle with reading had eye problems as babies. My ears pricked up. Harry had a squint, which I noticed when he was five months old. We took him to the doctor to have it checked, but were told he would grow out of it and, to be fair, to look at him now you would never know it had been an issue.

According to the optometrist, the legacy of this squint was that Harry's eyes were fighting against each other when he tried to read. Apparently, a person needs a lead eye to track correctly. Tracking is the technical term for being able to start at the left-hand side of a page and read across and down onto the next line without losing your place. If the child has a squint, they may never develop a lead eye. We took Harry along for his *Schoolvision* assessment, and two weeks later, at the end of January 2014, we picked up his special reading glasses. At Easter, Harry announced he was enjoying reading (to be honest, he rarely wants to read, but this made it easier). I felt like running around the neighbourhood shouting *Schoolvision*! Instead, I am committing our discovery to print. This is not a cure for dyslexia, but it may also be of help to your child. www.sportvision.co.uk/schoolvision/home.aspx

---

Top Fact 3

Having a squint as a baby may lead to

reading difficulties.

Top Tip 3

Find a behavioural optometrist who can check your child's

vision for Irlen Syndrome and if possible *Schoolvision.*

4. The Role of Memory

We now understand memory to be more than the ability to remember stuff; there are specialist areas within this field. I'm focusing on this because memory issues cause tremendous difficulties for people with dyslexia.

I have struggled with a poor memory all my life. I find it impossible to remember people's names or their faces. Harry has a similar problem. Now he's in secondary school, he has multiple teachers and always forgets their names. Two terms into the year, he still hasn't got a clue what any of his teachers are called.

DIANE, there's nothing more embarrassing than meeting someone you know well and forgetting their name. Worse still, if you meet them when you are with someone and have to make introductions. I've wanted the ground to swallow me up on numerous occasions when I couldn't for the life of me remember a good friend or neighbour's name.

Marie Rippel, who created, *All About Reading and All About Spelling,* has an excellent explanation of the different types of memory available in a free e-book called '*Help Your Child's Memory.*' Here is an affiliate link. https://bit.ly/3chYYdq

Short-term Memory

Most people with dyslexia have problems with short-term memory. Marie Rippel likens short-term memory to a funnel. If you put too much in, the narrow exit tube blocks. The key to making information stick is to only teach a child one concept or fact at a time. For example, when you are teaching your child a spelling word, teach the Long E spelt EA as in 'clear' and 'near' and make sure this is grasped before moving on to another letter blend. I have found Marie's resources excellent for Harry as they emphasise revision and regularly repeat the key concepts. School spelling tests rarely work for children with dyslexia. A one-off test is of little use in committing a new word to memory. I asked Harry's primary school teachers to reduce the number of words on his spelling tests and, whenever possible, he avoided taking them. We worked on his spelling at home using the *All About Spelling* programme. Working slowly and surely, and reviewing information at regular intervals, is the only way to prevent spelling words from being forgotten.

Working Memory

This is the ability to hold information in your head while you do something with it.

For example, a verbal maths problem may require the child to work out 5 x 6 and then add this answer to 50. The child needs to keep 50 in their head while they do the multiplication to get the answer 30. For a dyslexic, 50 will be swallowed by the dyslexia octopus during the first calculation. They don't have a hope of adding the two numbers to complete the problem.

Research shows that there are three types of memory:

- **Sensory memory** – this is where we store our first impressions of sights, sounds, and touch. Sensory memory is unlimited, and we can save vast amounts of sensory input
- **Long-term memory** – this is where we store information for long periods, anywhere from thirty seconds to a lifetime. Long-term memory is unlimited in capacity. When you teach, you want your child to store the information you introduce to their long-term memory.
- **Short-term memory** – this can be divided into **immediate memory** and **working memory.** Short-term memory is a temporary holding place for new information that comes in through sensory memory. This pays attention to the input and integrates it into long-term memory. Unlike sensory memory and long-term memory, short-term memory is quite limited in capacity.

Working memory is vital for school children. It is possible to strengthen working memory by playing memory games with your child. Do a web search for 'memory games' for ideas and play the old-fashioned game 'pairs' with them. There are now online options for this game.

www.webgamesonline.com/memory/

Processing Speed

This is nothing to do with any whizzy equipment on your kitchen bench. From memory (Wikipedia that is) processing speed refers to the time it takes a person to process the information they have been given when asked a question and to provide an answer. For those with slow processing speed, there can be a considerable lag between being asked a question and responding. This is not to say that the person is unintelligent. It all comes back to their mental filing system. Non-dyslexics can file the information away in an orderly manner in their brain. Multiplication facts are stored under basic mathematics facts; birthdays are stored under important dates, and so on. For a dyslexic person, there is no such filing system.

I, and many others with dyslexia, have a mental mattress. Information gets pushed under it, in whatever order it happened to arrive. When asked a question, the dyslexic person must mentally lift the mattress and, propping it up, do a quick shuffle around to find what they are looking for. Hence the delay. Therefore, timed tests are hopeless for a child with dyslexia and should be avoided. They only increase the child's sense of shame.

I can hear you saying, "That's nuts. People with dyslexia should just get themselves a decent filing system and be done with it." Oh, if only it were as simple as popping along to the local office suppliers and ordering a five-drawer filing cabinet with soft closing and a lockable top drawer. I can assure you if it were, the queue outside the shop door would be around the block. It's no fun having a bulging mental mattress. In fact, it's bloody hard work. When my son comes home from school, he is exhausted.

In the early years of school life, Harry couldn't manage any after-school activities. When he was six, I tried taking him to group piano lessons. He was very musical, forever singing and dancing around the house, and he was keen to learn the piano because his sister plays. The piano session for his age was at 3.30 pm on a Friday (what a dreadful time). By 4.00 pm, he was rolling around on the floor in the middle of the group holding his head. The poor thing's mental mattress was utterly overstuffed. Needless to say, we stopped going along to the lessons, and avoided all future activities at that time slot.

Top Fact 4

Due to their slow processing speed, timed tests are a disaster for children with dyslexia.

Top Tip 4

Respect the narrow input funnel and teach one concept at a time.

Play memory games with your child to

strengthen their working memory.

Educate your child's teacher about slow processing

speed and insist they don't use timed tests.

5. The Role of Sleep

While I remember, quality sleep is crucial for children with dyslexia because they are working much harder than other children to achieve the same results. Our children may even have to work harder while they sleep because they are trying to make sense of all the day's information they have randomly stuffed under their mental mattress.[26]

Sleep is now known to be as important as proper nutrition. Harry has always needed more sleep than other children of his age. If he has a late night, it is not pretty in our household the next day.

On the next page is the recommended amount of sleep all children require. Harry is fourteen and needs ten hours of sleep to be in top form. As I will discuss in Chapter Four, around 30% of children with dyslexia have ADD, according to the International Dyslexia Association.

Age	Hours of Sleep
0-1 yr	14-18hrs
1-3 yrs	12-14hrs
3-5 yrs	11-13hrs
5-12yrs	10-12hrs
12-18yrs	8.5-10hrs

ADD makes it very difficult for a child to switch off their brain at night. You may need to visit your doctor to get a prescription for melatonin or tart cherry tablets, which may help, these are not always available over the counter at a pharmacy.

I find stopping Harry's screen time an hour before bedtime and using a period of reading or listening to an audiobook helps him unwind before bed. We also don't allow phones, TV or computers in his bedroom at night. Yes, this is a constant battle, and we are apparently "the meanest parents in the world".

You can find out more about what supports good sleep in children at:

www.additudemag.com/sleep-aids-parents-children-adhd/

Top Fact 5

Children with dyslexia require more sleep than

their non-dyslexic peers.

Top Tip 5

Make sleep a priority for your child.

Insist upon a good bedtime routine and, if your child

struggles to get to sleep, investigate sleep aids

such as tart cherry or melatonin tablets.

---

6. Spelling and Reading Interventions

At this point, DIANE, I'd like to remind you we are still standing at an imaginary school gate (I'm sure our kids are giving us grief for chatting for soooo long).

I am a parent, not a teacher. Harry is now fourteen years old, and he's reading at the expected level for his age. Achieving this has taken years of extra support. My friend's six-year-old son was recently diagnosed with dyslexia. She asked if I had any tips on helping with reading. What follows is an account of the interventions we found helpful. I'm sure I've forgotten some (we tried so many) and just because they did or didn't work for Harry doesn't mean your child will have the same result. Remember those different types of dyslexia? Your child may have another form of dyslexia to Harry. Also, there are many resources we have not tried due to lack of time and funds. I appreciate everyone's budget is different. If you decide to invest in one of the following dyslexia programmes, I suggest you contact other parents who have used it to get a broader perspective.

Sharing my thoughts on these interventions is not to boast about what we've done. I know many parents have gone further. Marie Rippel, who I've already mentioned, wrote her own multi-sensory teaching programme for her dyslexic son. However, I have found personal recommendations helpful. As an excellent foundational resource, I recommend Abigail Marshall's book, *The Everything Parent's Guide to Children with Dyslexia*, especially Chapter 5, *Learning to Read*. I also found Ben Foss's *The Dyslexia Empowerment Plan* helpful in explaining why getting accommodations for your child is necessary. He likens information to water; in that it can come in different forms. Ben is severely dyslexic, and despite years of tuition with Orton-Gillingham (OG) programmes he is still in the bottom one per cent in his ability to name a letter. He does recommend the Orton-Gillingham approach but says,

"OG will not turn children with dyslexia into standard readers; it is more likely to help your child develop a somewhat stilted process for doing what other people do fluidly. To use a metaphor, it teaches them the most efficient way to crawl upstairs. This is better than not getting into the building at all, to be sure, but I still believe that a ramp is greatly preferable.[27]"

By 'ramp' he means using technology such as text-to-speech apps, audiobooks, digital pens and iPads to capture what is written on the board and to convert voice into text. He has an excellent chapter called *A Tool Kit of Accommodations*, which takes the reader through the various hardware and software available to help a dyslexic student. I found his book helpful in that it made me realise Harry requires extra help to get him to a literacy standard that enables him to function in the world. Once there, he still needs accommodations (such as text-to-speech, extra time in tests) for him to perform at a similar level to non-dyslexic students. There has never been a better time for students with dyslexia because there are numerous technology aids for reading and writing.

Orton-Gillingham will not turn children with dyslexia into standard readers; it is more likely to help your child develop a somewhat stilted process for doing what other people do fluidly.

For a comprehensive list of dyslexia programmes see: dyslexiahelp.umich.edu/tools/reading-programs

www.homeschoolingwithdyslexia.com/homeschool-language-arts-curriculum-dyslexia/

For a list of dyslexia apps see:

www.homeschoolingwithdyslexia.com/best-apps-dyslexia/

Be Your Child's Advocate

I appreciate some schools are doing incredible work teaching their dyslexic students; however, I cannot stress enough that concerned, supportive parents are often the difference between success and failure for a child with dyslexia. There is no quick fix. Each age brings new challenges. Sadly, you cannot assume employing a tutor or buying an online programme will be the answer. You must become your child's case manager. If dyslexia were a medical condition, such as diabetes, you would educate yourself and others about what your child needed. You must do the same for dyslexia. Be bold. Your child needs you to speak up when they are being penalised for having a learning difference. For example, Harry's primary school held an annual Spellathon – a fundraiser where children were sponsored to learn a list of twenty words. It was a very lucrative activity for the school. Most years, we opted out and gave a donation instead. The last thing I wanted was Harry humiliated in the name of raising funds.

Give your son or daughter a way of communicating their difficulties to teachers and peers without being embarrassed. I've encouraged Harry to say, "I have dyslexia. I'm improving, but I sometimes need help with my spelling and reading."

Insist on homework accommodations such as if the class is given three pages to read, your child is given one.

Read homework sheets out loud to your child. Investigate speech-to-text apps; Harry uses the free ones in *Google Docs* and *OneNote*. We have also had some success with audiobooks, which you can get from the library or companies such as *Audible.*

You must become your child's case manager. If dyslexia were a medical condition, such as diabetes, you would educate yourself and others about what your child needed.

I'm an *Audible* addict. I now choose to listen to, rather than read my book-club picks each month. In the past, I would have been too embarrassed to admit this, but I have changed my way of thinking, thanks to reading *The Dyslexia Empowerment Plan* by Ben Foss. He stressed that the information is what matters, not how a person acquires it. He talks about 'ear reading' versus 'eye reading'. I read a lot, and usually have three books on the go at any given time, but I read at the same speed I talk. Having read Ben Foss's chapter on reading speed, I discovered I am classed as a slow reader. Listening to audiobooks enables me to make good use of time when I'm gardening or driving, and it helps me 'read' longer books. I recently finished listening to *Mansfield Park* by Jane Austen, which took thirty-four hours. That would have been hard going for me to read.

If you own a scanner and a computer, school handouts can be scanned and sent to screen-reading software. I used to read Harry's homework to him before his reading reached its current standard. He still sometimes requires help to understand what questions mean, even though he can read them.

When Harry was younger, I insisted on a reader/writer for his tests, and he always excelled when he was given one. At home, I sometimes type up what he wants to say when he has a long piece of writing to produce, or he uses speech-to-text on *OneNote* or *Google Docs.*

If your child is in primary school, I suggest making an appointment to see your child's teacher at the beginning of each school year. I've never waited until the first parent/teacher evening. Arrange the meeting early on to discuss what your child needs to succeed. I suggest something along the following lines:

- Ask that your child sits near the front of the class.
- Insist other pupils don't mark your child's work.
- Request that the teacher never holds your child back at break or lunchtime to finish work.
- Suggest that oral testing be used if possible.
- Request your child be allowed to use technology.

If the school is unwilling to make accommodations, you may need to consider changing schools. Children are adaptable.

Harry has been to several schools, and it hasn't been a problem. In fact, it means when he goes to his sporting events he invariably knows someone.

Private Tutors

When Harry was in primary school, we were fortunate enough to be able to afford a private tutor for one hour per week. She'd trained in England and was qualified to teach dyslexic students. Harry was six years old, and he was too exhausted by the end of the day for extra tuition, so his school allowed me to take him to the tutor each Monday morning.

After some years, I switched to another tutor who was prepared to go into his school. This was slightly better in that it eliminated travel time. However, although I had been promised a room for his lesson, he often ended up having it in a corridor. His second tutor agreed to take Harry on because he had just turned eleven. In her opinion, dyslexic boys make more progress after this age as their brains are more receptive. I have no idea about the neuroscience behind this statement, but I noticed he did make more academic progress after he turned eleven.

In New Zealand, some parents opt for SPELD tutors. I didn't go down that route, but here's the link in case you wish to investigate this option: www.speld.org.nz.

Be aware that some after-school tutoring services have no

experience in teaching dyslexic students. They will take your money, but your child will not be getting specialist help. Ensure that any tutor you employ has a relevant experience in teaching children who have dyslexia.

The Steps Programme

In 2011, I attended a workshop given by the developer of the *Steps Programme*, Ros Lugg. She told the group how her work came about because she wanted to help her dyslexic husband and son. At that time, Harry was struggling with sequencing. He was often confused about the order of meals; he would get up in the morning and ask, "What's for lunch?" when he meant breakfast. He had no concept of the days of the week, or months of the year, and couldn't read an analogue clock. I purchased the *Steps* DVD and workbook for home use. He found it helpful and it did improve his sequencing issues but, because he already went to a tutor, I didn't buy the full programme.

Here is the website for the *StepsWeb*:

https://stepsweb.com/

Harry is now fourteen, and I've found it more challenging to work with him at home. He's less compliant as a teenager, so I'm taking him back to a specialist tutor for one hour per week. I'm pleased to see she uses the *Steps* resources and he is having success with them.

Davis Dyslexia Correction Programme

When Harry was seven, he still struggled to write his name; reading was torture. I was desperate. Around this time, I read Ronald D. Davis' book, *The Gift of Dyslexia*.[28] To give a little background to the author, in 1980, at the age of 38, Ron Davis discovered a way to overcome his dyslexia and found that the exercises he'd developed helped others. *The Davis Early Years Programme* involves making frequently used words (trigger words) out of clay. For example, the word 'in' might be depicted by a clay figure positioned under a clay archway. Next to this model would be a clay

arrow pointing through the arch. The word, 'in', also made from clay, would be placed beside the model. This would then be photographed, and the picture added to a file for future reference.

This process is time-consuming. There are hundreds of trigger words. The current Davis website states that the minimum age for the programme is eight. I now appreciate Harry was too young to benefit from the course.

Back in 2012, I paid $2,000 for the 30-hour programme. Harry got one helpful strategy. The facilitator began each session by throwing balls at him while he stood on one leg to catch them. She said this was to help him focus. I have to say it was a very costly game of catch. However, I have spoken to people who swear by the Davis Programme; I suspect they have a different type of dyslexia to Harry. If you are considering Davis, ask the facilitator for the contact details of three families they have worked with, and talk to them before signing up. The success of the programme is very dependent on the capability of the facilitator.

www.dyslexia.com/davis-difference/davis-programs/davis-reading-program-for-young-learners/

Fast ForWord

We ended up removing Harry from his primary school when he was six and a half. This was a big step. The school was local, and he had some lovely friends there, but I'm so glad we did. If we had kept him in that class, I believe his self-esteem would have been severely damaged. That year he had an inexperienced teacher. Literacy time consisted of her telling the children to write and putting a timer on for twenty minutes. The six-year-olds were expected to sit in silence, without any assistance, and produce written work. Harry, who couldn't write his name, became extremely distressed and eventually refused to go to school. I offered to go in every day to help him at literacy time, but the teacher wouldn't allow it. We withdrew Harry with the intention of home-schooling him, but I found a more play-based school, which suited his learning style.

That new school made use of a computer programme called *Fast ForWord,* to help their dyslexic students. Each day, Harry went out of class for a session on the computer. He also did ten minutes on our home computer in the evening. *Fast ForWord* did make a difference.

Unfortunately, Harry had to change school after a year, and the other school didn't use this programme. I looked into buying a private licence, but, on top of our tutoring bills, it was too costly for us. There do seem to be multiple ways to purchase *Fast ForWord* – if you are interested, it would pay to shop around.

www.fastforwordhome.com/what-is-fast-forword

Toe by Toe

When I investigated this, I liked the fact that Toe by Toe

is a systematic phonics programme. However, I suspected Harry would find it too dull, so I didn't use it. I do know of others who have had success with this programme. www.toe-by-toe.co.uk/what-is-toe-by-toe/

All About Learning Press

Marie Rippel, the developer of *All About Reading* and *All About Spelling,* is a woman after my own heart. When her son was nine, she was told by a paediatrician that he would never learn to read or spell. Not one to take failure as an option, she tried dozens of programmes and became desperate. Her son's difficulties in school made him act out to such an extent she was told he should be institutionalised. As a trained teacher, Marie was able to write her own multi-sensory programme based on the Orton Gillingham system to help him. For information about Orton Gillingham see this affiliate link: https://bit.ly/2FoRpWx

Using her resources, Marie's son overcame his dyslexia, so she decided to make them available to other parents. When I discovered her materials, Harry was ten, and his reading level was that of a six-year-old. I started him on *All About Spelling* Level 1, and we worked our way through the first three levels. The only time to do this was before school. I'd just read Barack Obama's autobiography *Dreams from my Father,* and had been impressed by his mother, who got him up at 5.30 a.m. to work with him before school. I knew that was too early for Harry – he needs his sleep – but we set a goal of working from 8 to 8.30 a.m. every weekday.

I can highly recommend *All About Learning's* resources. Visiting *All About Learning* via this affiliate link https:// bit.ly/3kFLUIj helps towards funding dyslexiaoctopus.com.

Marie's system uses magnetic tiles to build words. There are different colours for letter blends, vowels, prefixes and suffixes. We moved on from the spelling programme to *All About Reading*, and Harry worked his way through all the levels. My one reservation is that he didn't find the stories exciting as they are written primarily to teach a specific aspect of spelling. However, I would recommend this resource if you can work with your child regularly. People with dyslexia need to be systematically taught language that non-dyslexics just pick up.

Many schools have moved away from formal teaching of spelling rules. In Marie's programme, tips such as the letter 'c' says 's' before 'e', 'i' and 'y' helped Harry enormously. An older friend told me she was taught these hard and soft vowels at school. Sadly, this no longer seems to be the case, or if it is taught, it's mentioned once, and not repeated on a regular basis. Repetition is essential for a person with dyslexia due to their weak short-term memory.

One more tip about reading. I try to get Harry to read for fifteen to twenty minutes each evening. This isn't easy. He hasn't found any genre that has gripped him. Knowing his passion for mountain biking, I recently bought him some books and magazines on the topic. Engrossed in his latest bike magazine, he asked me if he could read for another ten minutes; my heart is still singing!

For Marie Rippel's free dyslexia resources use this affiliate link: https://bit.ly/30gKISQ

Sound Therapy

When Harry had his speech therapy, his therapist always sat on his right side. I asked why, and was told the sound processing centre is on the left side of the brain, which connects to the right side of the body.

Remember the lead eye section? Well, it turns out the right ear should be the lead ear. If a student is left-ear dominant, there is a small delay in auditory processing. Sounds captured by the left ear must cross the central bundle of nerves connecting the two sides of the brain to get to the auditory processing area in the left hemisphere. This creates a processing delay.[29]

In 2012, I went to hear Professor Gail Gillon from the University of Canterbury give a public lecture entitled, 'What if we can prevent dyslexia'. This can be found on YouTube https://youtu.be/ZzyZquJ4260

In her talk, Professor Gillon talked about her research into sound therapy. Children who had been identified as having problems with reading were played special tapes which trained their ears to hear certain pitches. I noticed when I moved to New Zealand, that there is a difference between countries in the sounds that people can hear.

According to sound therapist Alfred Tomatis:[30]

"Every ethnic ear can be defined by its spectrum of receptivity... The French ear, for example, hears between 1,000 and 2,000hz... British ear between 2,000 and 12.000hz...the North American ear between 750 and 3,000hz... This does not mean that in each of these examples, there is deafness to frequencies outside the

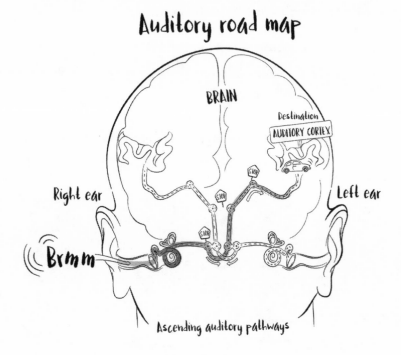

Auditory road map

basic frequency band. But an undeniable sensitivity to certain frequencies exists which explains the under-use of other frequencies..."

Dr Tomatis believes left-ear dominance leads to longer processing time, hesitant or broken speech, monotone voice, difficulties reading out loud, and poor reading comprehension. I purchased a piece of equipment called Forbrain from Tomatis New Zealand.

Forbrain is a headset which allows the user to hear their own voice as others hear it. Harry did not find this device helpful, but some people swear by it. I suspect I discovered it too late as Harry's speech therapy tutor had already corrected his speech issues. I am currently investigating other aspects of the Tomatis method in the hope it will help Harry's auditory processing issues.

To finish my story about Professor Gillon's work, she found that pre-school children could be identified as having weak phonological awareness by getting them to play a special computer game. Once identified, they were given support. I found the lecture's title provocative, as the intervention doesn't prevent dyslexia, which is a brain wiring difference. Still, it may reduce the severity of the condition if picked up early.

Cellfield

As mentioned earlier, DIANE, I have gathered much of the helpful information about dyslexia from chatting with other parents. This was the case with *Cellfield*. Sitting next to another mother at the end-of-year orchestral concert, we fell into conversation about high school options. She asked me why I had chosen the one Harry was to go to. I said it was because it had a dyslexia unit and a teacher aid in each class. Her eyes lit up. It turned out that her daughter also had dyslexia. She shared with me that the *Cellfield* programme had made a massive difference to her daughter's reading ability, and she promptly texted me the tutor's number.

I booked Harry in for the programme. As he was drawing near to the end of primary school, I knew he wouldn't miss much if he took an hour and a half out of school every morning for two weeks. Before the programme began, the tutor tested his reading level, and I also had his eyesight tested by a behavioural optometrist because the programme claims to improve eye tracking. I was keen to see if it made any measurable improvements. He went at 9 a.m. every morning for ten days and had fifteen minutes of *Cellfield* homework each evening.

The *Cellfield* programme is computer-based. Harry had to wear special glasses to complete the on-screen exercises. The homework reading material looked like gobbledegook to me, but in fact, each word had its beginning and final letter swapped around and an additional letter 'a' on the end, for example, he had to decode *hortsa appyha oyba*, which is *short happy boy*. This approach forced him to study each word carefully. Harry also had to learn homophones (words which sound the same but are spelt differently, for example 'week' and 'weak'). He had no problem with these because he'd learned them in *All About Spelling*.

At the end of the programme, his Word Attack ability had jumped from nine years to seventeen years. His Comprehension ability went from ten years to thirteen years, and he could read more fluently. When I had his eyes re-tested, his focal length and eye-tracking had both improved.

I think, for once, I got this intervention at the perfect time. I wanted to boost Harry's confidence before high school, and his improved results certainly achieved this. The tutor recommended he continue to read for twenty minutes every night for three months. This gave me an excuse to make him read right through the six-week summer holidays. When he began high school, he transitioned smoothly.

We paid $2,000, and I had to be available to transport him between the appointments and school. However, I believe *Cellfield* did make a difference. Six months on, Harry had not been good at reading every night. He was re-tested by the tutor and had slipped back slightly but was still far above where he had been before the course. After a follow-on two terms of weekly tutoring, he gained back what he had lost and made further improvements. This gave him the spur to get back into regular reading. As ever, it is a case of use it or lose it!

www.cellfield.com

Mind Mapping

In 2009, I attended a workshop in Christchurch by Neil MacKay, a UK dyslexia expert. He taught several strategies to help children study. One of them was mind mapping. I had come across Tony Buzan, the father of mind mapping, several years earlier. I ordered one of Buzan's books, *Mind Mapping Mastery*[31] from the local library, and when Harry had an English project, we planned it using the mind mapping technique. Harry was pleased with the way he could finally get his thoughts down using symbols and pictures. Mind mapping may be helpful for your child if they are upper primary age or older.

For Mind Mapping see:

Mind Maps for Kids: An Introduction The Shortcut to Success at School by Tony Buzan ISBN 9780007151332

For Neil MacKay see:
www.actiondyslexia.co.uk.

Top Fact 6

Children need to be taught language that non-dyslexic children just pick up. Orton Gillingham-based programmes are effective because they are systematic, they can be done at home, or you can employ a tutor who uses this approach.

Top Tip 6

Expecting a main-stream school to provide your child with all the support they require to learn to read and spell may be unrealistic. Children with dyslexia need a considerable amount of help. Whatever your budget, any assistance you can provide is well worth the investment of time and money. It's never too late to help your child, but the earlier you start, the better.

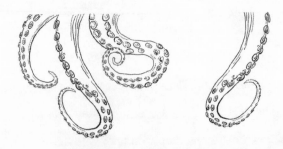

Chapter Four

Oh, say can you say (if this is related to dyslexia)

Associated Learning and Health Challenges

Something no dyslexia assessor ever mentioned to me when discussing Harry is the close correlation between dyslexia and other learning challenges. I've had to research this topic for myself. As the focus of this book is dyslexia, I am only going to touch on these other learning challenges to bring them to your attention. If you suspect one or more of these other conditions may be a problem for your child, you may wish to do further research. Remember, labels are not harmful; they give you the power to know how best to help your child.

In this chapter, DIANE, I will share what has helped our

family with our health. Research has shown many people with dyslexia suffer from similar health conditions, and I trust this information will be of use to you.

Disclaimer.

It is important to note that a child's diet should not be modified or changed drastically without consulting with their paediatrician. When considering new supplements, always consult with your child's physician, especially if your child is taking other medication.

What is the Definition of the Term 'Learning Difficulty'?

I like the following definition:

"A learning difficulty is a condition that can cause an individual to experience problems in a traditional classroom learning context. It may interfere with literacy skills development and math/maths and can also affect memory, ability to focus and organizational skills. A child or adult with a learning difficulty may require additional time to complete assignments at school and can often benefit from strategy instruction and classroom accommodations, such as material delivered in special fonts or the ability to use a computer to take notes.

No two individuals with a learning difficulty are exactly alike and many conditions, such as dyslexia, attention deficit disorder, attention deficit hyperactive disorder, dyscalculia, and dysgraphia, exist on a wide spectrum. There is also dyspraxia, a motor-skills difficulty that can affect a learner's ability to write by hand and may impact on planning skills. It's not uncommon for learning difficulties and motor-skills difficulties to co-present. For example, dyslexia and dyspraxia, or ADD/ADHD and dyspraxia can occur together.

Learning difficulties are sometimes referred to as learning disabilities. You may also encounter the terms learning differences or specific learning differences. The differences between these labels can seem subtle but may have implications for how an individual with a learning difficulty views him or herself. The word disability implies a person is less able than his or her peers. It can also suggest they are in a permanent state of disadvantage and cause them to lose agency.

On the other hand, a learning difference takes the opposite approach in underscoring that a person simply learns in a different way from others. They are not disabled, it's just that their brains work differently. The term learning difficulty falls somewhere in-between, describing the added challenges an individual might face in a typical school environment, but also suggesting that these challenges are difficulties that can be overcome.[32]"

Overlapping Learning Challenges

At school, I never understood all those long-winded maths problems about people digging holes and sharing out bags of sweets – surely life is too short to worry about such things? The only aspect of maths I did enjoy was Venn Diagrams. In case you haven't got a clue what I'm going on about, Venn diagrams are a pictorial representation of a maths problem using overlapping circles. I love drawing and colouring, and they gave me an excuse to whip out my coloured pencils to shade the overlapping segments.

A person with dyslexia often resembles a Venn diagram. Their overlapping difficulties may include reading, spelling, mathematics, memory, information processing, direction, poor dexterity, poor time management and navigation difficulties, sensory sensitivity to noise and impaired social skills.

On the following page is an illustration of this as an ice cream where the flavours are the various challenges. Recently, while on holiday with a friend, we went to buy an ice cream. The cabinet was well stocked and as I pored over my options, my friend ordered a vanilla cone. I was shocked. So many options and he had just picked boring vanilla! In my mind, a person with dyslexia is like that ice cream cabinet. There are no vanilla dyslexics – other flavours will always be present.

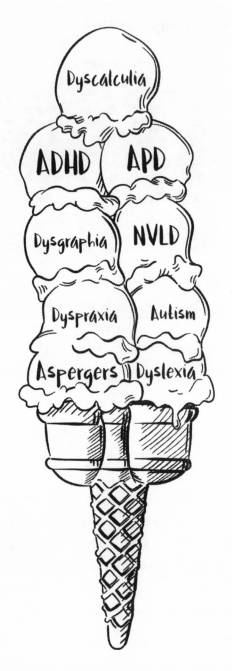

The following is a guide to what other learning challenges may look like in primary school children. If you recognise your child as having these characteristics, you may like to make further investigation.

ADD/ADHD

About 30% of people who have dyslexia also have attention deficit disorder (ADD) or attention deficit hyperactivity disorder.[33]

These days the term ADD tends to cover both conditions. Harry has ADD, and I recognise some ADD tendencies in myself. However, the challenge is to know where dyslexia ends and ADD begins.

Healing ADD by Daniel G Amen[34] is a fascinating book. I highly recommend it if your child has this condition. Typically, people with ADD have the following symptoms:

- **Short attention span.** Short attention span for mundane, everyday tasks. However, people with ADD can focus on tasks for long periods if the tasks are engaging or exciting.

- **Distractibility.** People with ADD are highly sensitive to their environment. Light, sounds, smells, certain tastes, or even clothing they are wearing, can distract them.

- **Disorganisation.** Mess and disorder are standard features in the lives of people with ADD. Keeping possessions and spaces tidy is a constant battle, and efficiently filing paperwork is challenging. Timekeeping is a weakness; people with ADD are frequently late and miss deadlines.

- **Procrastination.** Pulling all-nighters is normal for people with ADD, who wait until the last moment before starting a task or project. They often wait until people nag them before they get things done.

- **Poor internal supervision.** Poor executive function is a symptom of ADD. This leads to poor judgment and low impulse control. Often people with ADD say or do things without considering the consequences. They also have a harder time learning from their mistakes.

Dr Amen has categorised seven types of ADD. His book helped me understand the challenges Harry faces. An excellent website for learning more about ADD and ADHD is additudemag.com.

I am a member of ADHD New Zealand and get their helpful quarterly newsletter. Parenting a child with ADD or ADHD is very demanding; you need all the support you can get. I would recommend connecting to your local or national ADHD association. A word of caution, I am a member of various Facebook groups for dyslexia and ADD and often pick up useful information and strategies from their pages. Be aware, however, these groups can be negative at times. Some parents, overwhelmed by their children's needs, use online forums to vent their frustrations. If you are feeling down, it may not be the time to check these out.

About 30% of people who have dyslexia also have attention deficit disorder (ADD) or attention deficit hyperactivity disorder. (International Dyslexia Association)

Auditory Processing Disorder

Harry had difficulty understanding vowel sounds when he was young, and we had his hearing tested on several occasions. In Harry's most recent dyslexia testing, we were told he does have auditory processing disorder (APD). The assessor said all children who have ADD have a degree of APD. A University of Auckland study confirms this. It found 94% of children with APD also had a language impairment and/or a reading disorder.[35] Kids with APD have a hard time getting jokes, following the rules in a game, and keeping up with conversations.

People with APD may struggle with:

- **Picking up the subtlety in sounds**. To some children with APD, all voices sound the same.
- **Being able to distinguish between background sounds and speech.** For example, noise from an air-conditioning unit can make it difficult for a child to pick up the teacher's voice.
- **Recalling what was said**. When a problem arises in the playground, and a teacher asks what happened, a child with APD will struggle to remember the correct order of what was said.

Bear in mind children with APD will pass a standard hearing test. Only a trained audiologist can conduct the tests needed to diagnose APD.

Dyspraxia

Dyspraxia is a disorder of gesture.[36] You might hear people describe these problems using two different names. Dyspraxia is one, developmental coordination disorder (DCD) is the other. These terms are slightly different, but they describe many of the same difficulties.

Dyspraxia refers to trouble with movement. That includes difficulty in four essential areas:

- **Fine motor skills** – using small muscles in the hands and wrists for tasks like writing, drawing and cutting.
- **Gross motor skills** – large movements like climbing

and jumping.

- **Motor planning** – remembering how to carry out repetitive actions like brushing teeth.
- **Coordination** – affects crawling, walking, dressing and playing sports.

For more information, contact your national Dyspraxia Association. In New Zealand this is dyspraxia.org.nz

Dysgraphia

Dysgraphia is a problem that affects a person's ability to write. The signs include:

1. **Poor letter formation.** Learning how to create letters from curves and lines is a struggle. Lower case letters are the most challenging as they are made up of more curved lines and are smaller. Reversed letters or writing in only capital letters is typical.

2. **Pain and frustration from handwriting.** Children with dysgraphia find writing painful. A child may awkwardly position their wrist and elbow and not be able to hold a pencil using the tripod grip. They may struggle to apply the correct pressure when writing, and the paper can slip away from them.

3. **Text incorrectly spaced.** A child may find it hard to create the correct space between letters, words, and sentences. The writing may run into the margins. They

will struggle to fill in boxes on worksheets or forms.

4. **Poor spelling.** The effort required to form letters means that spelling mistakes are more likely to occur. Planning and producing grammatically correct sentences can be difficult for a child with dysgraphia.

5. **Ungrammatical and disorganized writing.** Run-on sentences are common, and misuse or lack of punctuation may show up. Written work does not reflect verbal ability.

6. **Avoidance of schoolwork.** Writing difficulties affect all areas of learning and can lead to unfinished classwork and a reluctance to do homework.

7. **Low confidence and a negative self-image.** As with other specific learning differences, dysgraphia can cause plummeting confidence and poor self-esteem.[37]

If you suspect your child has dysgraphia here is a useful link from the International Dyslexia Association.

https://dyslexiaida.org/understanding-dysgraphia/

Dyscalculia

When I worked as a Saturday girl (DIANE, I know it's hard to believe I got the job I mentioned in the Prologue), being on the till at the front of the shop petrified me. Customers would hand me their purchases and wait until I'd rung them through before saying, "Oh, and I'll also take a packet of

Marlboros and a newspaper."

Tills back then were basic. I'd have to add up the extra purchases in my head and work out their change. Terrifying! I can still feel the shame of being unable to do this with a queue stretching the length of the shop. I salute all those who work in retail; it's not my forte.

Percentages make me sweat. I survived mathematics at school by sitting next to the cleverest girl and copying her answers. My husband is mathematically gifted, and therefore he is the go-to parent for maths homework. Harry is good at maths but sometimes struggles to understand the questions if they are written out as long-winded problems.

I was surprised to read 50–60% of dyslexics have difficulty with maths.[38] Few maths teachers I have come across are aware of this. For some students, dyslexia makes it difficult to read mathematical questions, but for others, the problem is dyscalculia, which is an impediment in mathematics.

Basic Maths Facts (The dreaded times tables!)

Do you know what one of the most challenging tasks is for a child with dyslexia? TIMES F***ING TABLES!

Mathematics teachers are obsessed with times tables. Sadly, little has changed in this regard since I was at school. I can clearly remember the stomach-churning anxiety of times tables tests. I struggled with my seven and eight times tables. When I was nine years old, my teacher thought it was hilarious to tell us we needed to learn the thirteen times table over a weekend. I slaved away all day Saturday and Sunday and hardly slept. On Monday morning, he told the class he'd been joking. To me, this was another example of the tyranny of school.

I read that Diane Swonk, an internationally recognised chief economist and financial commentator, couldn't memorise her times tables at school due to her dyscalculia.[39] This, along with her other dyslexia challenges, left her with an abiding feeling of insecurity. However, she had absolutely no difficulty understanding algebra and calculus. This fact is important because at my son's primary school the maths teacher refused to let my friend's child progress in maths until he had mastered the times tables. His various learning challenges, including dyslexia, prevented him from memorising them. I wanted to yell, "For Heaven's sake! Just give the kid a copy of the tables!"

Harry's short-term memory had no way of holding the answers to the times tables. We tried for years and got nowhere.

Marie Rippel on *All About Learning Press* explains that the brain must make connections with what it already knows to retain information.

"Knowledge is organised into elaborate networks called schemas... As your child's brain builds a schema, new information is attached to previously stored information... If there is nothing to relate the new information to, there is no way for it to be stored in long-term memory. Instead, it is dropped from short-term memory and completely forgotten. If someone talks to you in Russian, and you don't speak Russian, there is nothing for that information to connect to, and the information is dropped.[40]"

A piece of research comparing instructional methods in middle schools saw one group of students taught about the Holocaust with traditional teaching methods: lecturing, group discussion, and visual resources, and a second group studied the same material using a multisensory approach.[41] The students in the second group achieved higher scores in all subsequent testing.

Teaching in a multisensory way involves using sight, sound, and touch. Combining all three pathways with simultaneous multisensory instruction is called the SMI method. It is powerful because brain neurons that fire together, wire together. This is what the Davis method is doing in making clay words. I found adding pictures and story to the times tables made a huge difference to Harry. Numbers are abstract, which makes them hard to remember, whereas images, being concrete, are relatively simple for the brain to store and retrieve.

Harry is a picture thinker, as are most people with dyslexia. I was delighted to find a resource on multiplication.com which uses pictures and stories to teach the times tables.

shoe X skate = sick queen

2 8 16

Each number is represented by a picture: 2 = shoe, 3 = tree, and so on. A story is then written around the two numbers interacting. For example, 2 x 8 is shown as a shoe and a skate. In the story a queen wearing one shoe and one skate spins around until she is dizzy, i.e. she becomes a sick queen.

Therefore: shoe x skate = sick queen. 2 x 8 = 16.

Each story is illustrated, and because of this, Harry can remember them. I read through each story a couple of times and showed Harry the illustrations. That was enough for him to remember the answers. Please note, there isn't a story for 10, 11 and 12 times tables. The 10 and 11 are easier for children to remember, and in countries which use metric measurements, there is less necessity for children to know the 12 times table.

I can't promise this story system will work for your child, but if it does, I know you will be as thrilled as I was.

www.multiplication.com/teach/teach-the-times-tables

For a helpful overview of dyscalculia see:

www.understood.org/en/learning-attention-issues/child-learning-disabilities/dyscalculia/understanding-dyscalculia

I also recommend checking out the British Dyslexia Association website, which has some helpful information on dyscalculia.

www.bdadyslexia.org.uk/dyslexic/maths-difficulties-dyscalculia

What O'clock?

Time is fluid for me and for many people with dyslexia. Learning to tell the time can prove challenging. Harry struggled to master the analogue clock and prefers digital displays, whereas I need a watch with a clock face. Digital time displays don't give me a sense of urgency. I can see that it's 8.55 but only by looking at clock hands do I appreciate it's almost nine o'clock. It will seem strange to someone who doesn't have dyslexia, that a person can read the clock face but have no grasp of time. I also find the twenty-four-hour clock extremely difficult and hate flight timetables. I must do the maths every time to work out what 13.40 or 15.07 means.

On the topic of time, the most useful device in our household is a small magnetic timer that lives on our fridge. It can set it to count up or down. Ten minutes to spare before an appointment used to be a recipe for disaster. Having no concept of what I could realistically achieve in ten minutes, I got lost in a large task and end up running late. Now I set the timer for ten minutes and, here's the cunning part, I leave it in another room. This forces me to stop whatever I'm doing when the alarm goes off. It works a treat. The timer has also helped us set healthy parameters on Harry's screen time. He gets lost in a computer game and thirty minutes flashes by. The use of a timer reduces my need to nag.

The timer functions on a smartphone is are also beneficial. Harry has an alarm set for ten minutes before his saxophone lesson. This is the only way he has a hope of getting to it.

Travel time is also a tough concept for someone with dyslexia. My being habitually late drives my husband crazy. To me, on time means anywhere up to ten minutes past the agreed time. To him, it means arriving early. It's taken me years to not leave the house at the time I am supposed to arrive. I've finally put in place a system of going fifteen minutes earlier than I expect the journey to take.

In researching dyslexia, I discovered struggling with being on time has a technical name. I always thought it was 'being hopeless', but in fact, it is 'temporal-sequential disorganisation' and is an aspect of executive functioning common to people with dyslexia.

As an aside, there's a medical term for the chaos in the kitchen when I cook. It is 'material-spatial disorganisation' (if only I could remember that long name when my mother-in-law rolls her eyes at my dinner-time disasters).

Other Learning Challenges

The list of learning challenges which overlap with dyslexia is long. If you Google the work of Mary Colley, you'll find helpful diagrams of neurodiversity issues. I don't have the training to do justice to them all, but they include:

- Nonverbal learning disorder
  www.additudemag.com/what-is-nonverbal-learning-
  disorder-symptoms-and-diagnosis/
- Developmental coordination disorder (DCD)
  www.understood.org/en/learning-attention-issues/
  child-learning-disabilities/dyspraxia/understanding-
  developmental-coordination-disorder-dcd
- Autism - www.autismnz.org.nz/
- Asperger's
  Child Development Institute
  https://archive.ph/NLbHu Archived webpage

Getting a professional assessment is essential. You may require a few different assessments to get to the bottom of your child's learning difficulties.

Top Fact 7

Children with dyslexia will also have some other learning challenges in varying degrees.

Top Tip 7

Investigate what other learning challenges your child may have and find out what support you can access.

Health Challenges

The Genetics of Dyslexia – Skin Conditions and Allergies

Due to the overlapping nature of learning difficulties, it is often tricky to identify which health challenges are purely due to dyslexia. What is clear is that dyslexia is a genetic condition and researchers are having some success in isolating the genes responsible. More studies are required to understand the genetic component of dyslexia. One known gene is found on chromosome 6. This chromosome is also responsible for, amongst other things, immunity. The following extract is taken from www.dyslexic.org.uk/research/genetics-dyslexia

"After the identification of the chromosome 6 and 18 sites we have focused our attention on pinpointing the actual genes responsible for reading impairment. Our initial strategy has been to specifically target genes that we knew to be expressed in the brain. The analysis of about 50 genetic markers within 15 brain-expressed genes located on chromosome 6 revealed strong associations between one gene, named KIAA0319, and low performance in most of our tests for reading, spelling, orthography and phonology. We replicated this result in a sample of US families and the same association was picked up in a completely independent analysis carried out at Cardiff University.

KIAA0319 has turned out to be involved with controlling the early development of the brain. It may also underlie the unfortunate tendency of the immune system of dyslexics to cause allergies, eczema etc."

A UK study has identified gene DCDC2 gene, also found on chromosome 6, has a part to play in dyslexia.[42]

The Dyslexia Research Trust is a useful site: www.dyslexic.org.uk/ They have a section on immunology. The following is a quote from this page.

"As many parents know all too well, dyslexic children and their families tend to be prone to allergies, such as skin rashes, eczema and asthma. These conditions are due to the body producing antibodies which attack your own skin or lungs for some reason. They are much more common in dyslexics. The development of magnocells is under the control of the immune gene complex on chromosome 6.[43]"

I suffer from contact dermatitis, and I know other dyslexics who have psoriasis and eczema. I have not been able to find any studies which estimate the percentage of people with dyslexia who also have skin conditions, but the link is well known. Asthma and hay fever are also common in people who have dyslexia.

As a child, I was prescribed strong steroid creams for my

dermatitis and this exacerbated my other health conditions. These days, to control my dermatitis, I have removed chemical products such as detergents and household cleaners from our home. I do my housework with microfibre cloths and water. Washing dishes with standard dishwashing liquid always wrecked my hands if I didn't wear gloves. Plant-based liquids don't irritate my skin and my hands no longer require protection. However, I always wear gloves when gardening as soil is a major irritant for me.

One known gene for dyslexia is found on chromosome 6. This chromosome is also responsible for, amongst other things, immunity.

Food Intolerances

The Gut

The gut has become a hot topic in health. You'll often hear the gut called 'the second brain'. The gut is responsible for 80% of a person's immunity (health24.com). It seems plausible to me that just as people with dyslexia have structural differences in their brains, they may have anomalies in their 'second brain', the gut.

For a comprehensive list of symptoms that can be caused by food allergies see:

https://archive.ph/VNaAgn Archived webpage.

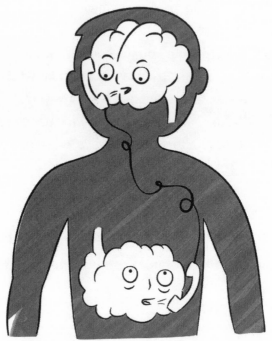

Coeliac Disease and Gluten Sensitivity

Harry was a difficult baby. He had colic, reflux, and drew his legs up to his chest in pain after drinking his milk. As previously mentioned, he was enormous at birth – way above the 99 percentile. However, things changed once he started solids.

Harry was never interested in puréed food. When I presented him with pumpkin, apple or other fruit and veggies, he would shut his mouth as tight as a trap, whereas he watched his dad chomping away on a piece of meat he would try to grab the fork. We took the hint and started him on finger food.

He loved it.

When Harry was ten months old, we made an extended trip back to the UK to introduce him to our relatives. In a fit of madness, we toured the length and breadth of the British Isles and stayed in over thirty different homes (what were we thinking!). Having to go along with what our hosts were eating, Harry mainly ate fish fingers, sausages and bananas. He also transitioned from formula to normal cow's milk. Throughout the trip, he screamed most nights and his poos were horrific.

DIANE, if you're eating, you may wish to skip this bit. How can I describe his nappies? Think of a cross between stinking pond slime and pea soup. I took him to a doctor in England to have a stool test done because I thought he had dysentery. The test came back negative, and the doctor's only suggestion was that he was reacting to different tap water.

On our flight back to New Zealand we went through four changes of clothes because of Harry's horrendous diarrhoea. To top off that memorable flight, I caught food poisoning from the in-flight chicken meal and vomited. Not surprisingly, I stuff this memory at the bottom of my mental mattress.

Back in New Zealand, I visited four different doctors, and even took Harry to the hospital, desperate to get an answer to what was causing his diarrhoea. My lack of success via conventional medicine led me to see a homoeopath. Can you hear the cash register ringing, DIANE? On her advice, we removed cow's milk and put him onto goat's milk along with some homoeopathic remedies. The change in milk did make him calmer, but he still caught a cold every three to four weeks and had a constantly snotty nose, which was much worse than the norm for a teething child.

When Harry was almost three, I became concerned that he was frequently saying "Ow!" and rubbing his legs. We went to see a naturopath (more $$$s) who suggested removing gluten from his diet. We did this, and then decided to take him to a private paediatrician who specialised in gluten sensitivity (yet more $$$s). The paediatrician gave him a blood test which showed that he carried the coeliac gene and had markers for gluten sensitivity.

Here's a bit of guff about the coeliac gene. Apparently, 95% of people with coeliac disease have the HLA-DQ2 gene, and most of the remaining 5% have the HLA-DQ8 gene.[44] Genetic testing can determine if you have one or both. Having the gene means you are at risk for developing coeliac disease, but you won't definitely get it. However, a negative result virtually rules out coeliac disease but not gluten sensitivity.

What the Heck is Gluten?
- Gluten is a food protein found in wheat, rye and barley.
- It is very often hidden in processed foods such as meat

at the deli counter. (Flour is used as a thickener and binder, and meat is sometimes pumped with gluten.)
- Some food additives are made from gluten-containing grains, check for wheat starch in any list of ingredients.

Coeliac disease (American spelling celiac) is caused by a reaction of the immune system to gluten. When someone with coeliac disease eats gluten, their gut lining is damaged, and this leads to decreased absorption of nutrients. It is estimated that one in 100 people have coeliac disease. However, only 30% of people are successful in getting a diagnosis.[45]

"Hold on," I hear you shout. "You're one of those mad crusaders thumping on about the need for a gluten-free world, aren't you?"

Please understand I'm not saying every person with dyslexia has coeliac disease or is gluten sensitive, but many do have an issue with gluten. The following is from a 1997 study. "After screening 291 pupils in the fourth grade, 15 dyslexic and 15 controls were pairwise matched by gender, age and cognitive level. Word decoding, spelling, and short-term memory tests were carried out, and information on handedness, immune and other disorders was obtained." Blood and urine tests were taken for each group. The study found, "the reading abilities significantly differentiated the groups, and significant differences were found in frequency of left-handedness, immune disorders and other disorders.

Three dyslexic children had elevated IgA antibodies. Two of these had positive endomycium tests, and coeliac disease was confirmed by biopsy. One had antibodies to proteins in milk. Our findings may suggest weak urinary peptide abnormalities in the dyslexic children, and they show significant differences in the levels of IgA of antibodies to food proteins.[46]"

Dr Rodney Ford M.D. is a children's doctor (paediatrician) based in Christchurch, New Zealand. He believes gluten damages the brain and nerve cells of susceptible people.

A 2018 review of research found that the rate of coeliac disease in the global population is 1.4%.[47] Of course, because so many coeliacs and dyslexics are undiagnosed, it is impossible to put an accurate figure on this, but the rate of coeliac disease is much higher for people with dyslexia than the general population.

"One hundred and five dyslexic and 105 control children were compared for frequency of immune diseases, autoimmune diseases, and non-righthandedness in the light of the Geschwind-Behan (1982) 'testosterone hypothesis'. The results showed significantly more immune and autoimmune-diseases in the dyslexic group.[48]"

Probably the first epidemiological study of gluten intolerance consisted of an informal survey of about twenty people with gluten-related sensitivity and found over 90% reported improvement from a gluten-free diet.[49] All spoke of delayed learning prior to a gluten-free diet, either in themselves, or their children. Some of the physiological, cognitive, and emotional symptoms they reported with dietary avoidance of gluten included:

- Improved ability to learn
- Improved interest in school
- Improved concentration
- No need to continue with meds for depression
- Improved physical growth (previously was smaller than average)
- Found a "hunger" for learning after avoiding gluten
- Improved mood with less "crossness" and "crankiness"
- Improved intellect with definite increases in intelligence
- Improved speed of learning
- No more "brain fog"
- Noticeable improvement in reading

Before going gluten-free, students had the following difficulties/complaints:

- Daydreaming in school
- Difficulty in finishing sentences and finding words
- Speech delay
- In and out of Special Education classes
- Delays in walking and talking
- Vitamin deficiencies

- Short-term and long-term memory were poor
- Anxiety problems
- Tummy aches

Having seen the list, I think you will agree it's worth investigating whether gluten is an issue for your child.

I mentioned problems with gluten to a friend whose daughter was tiny for her age. My friend said, "Oh, she can't be gluten-intolerant or have coeliac disease; she loves bread so much."

Fortunately, she listened to my explanation that people who have coeliac disease may enjoy eating bread and cakes; it's just that these foods are damaging to their health. She did get her child tested, and she came back positive. Since removing gluten, her daughter is thriving.

You may not be aware that gluten affects more than the bowel. The following is a list of less well-known consequences of eating gluten:

- **Speech.** One surprising aspect of removing gluten was that Harry's speech, which at almost three still hadn't gone further than a few words, took off within weeks. The paediatrician told us that this is not uncommon because gluten can affect mental capacity.
- **Weight gain.** Once off gluten, Harry began to put on weight, which was a huge relief, because he had only gained one kilo in his second year of life. The poor kid

looked like a length of string with two knots tied in it for his knees.

- **Bedwetting.** Harry didn't suffer from this, but I have read that gluten may also be behind bedwetting as it inflames the bladder and makes it impossible for a person to know when their bladder is full.

If you suspect that your child may have a gluten issue, these are some of the common symptoms:

- Large, bulky, foul-smelling stools or diarrhoea or constipation
- Poor weight gain
- Weight loss in older children
- Chronic anaemia
- Stunted growth
- Abdominal distension, pain and flatulence
- Nausea and vomiting
- Tiredness or lack of stamina
- Hyperactivity or cranky or grumpy
- Skin bruises easily
- Bone and joint pain
- Difficulty in concentrating on a task

Symptoms can only occur once gluten is part of a child's diet. Often people develop these problems much later in life. According to the Coeliac Society in the UK, many people are diagnosed between the ages of forty and sixty, and it takes on average thirteen years to get a coeliac diagnosis.[50]

Thirteen years!

Shocking though this is, it doesn't surprise me. No doctor picked up my gluten issues despite me having several autoimmune conditions and suffering from infertility. I feel very fortunate that we have a specialist in our city who understands coeliac disease. It only took us a year to get to the root of Harry's problems.

People have told me on many occasions that Harry will grow out of his coeliac disease. Sadly, having read extensively around this subject, I know that children with coeliac disease need to maintain a strict gluten-free diet for life. If Harry does this, he can live an active, healthy life like anyone else.

But a word of caution; don't remove gluten before you've had a blood test for gluten markers. Be aware that the doctor might say the blood results are fine. My son's doctor said his blood results were normal. Only when we went to the specialist did we get an accurate test. However, a visit to your GP is the correct place to start. The official path for being diagnosed with coeliac disease is:

- Visit the doctor and have the blood test done **before** stopping eating gluten.
- Have a biopsy of the bowel

Pathway to a Coeliac Diagnosis

1 Visit your GP for a blood test. You must be eating gluten containing foods for an accurate result.

2 Appointment with gastroenterologist. Do not remove gluten from your diet before a biopsy of the gut is taken.

3 Consult a dietitian for advice on gluten free eating.

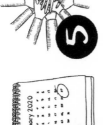

4 Have an annual blood test to check essential nutrients are being absorbed.

5 Join your national coeliac society for ongoing support.

It's worth doing this correctly because in many countries subsidies are available to offset the cost of gluten-free food.

For gluten sensitivity, experts recommend you first get tested for a wheat allergy and then for coeliac disease. If both are negative, try an elimination diet. Removing gluten for a month will give you an indication of how it is affecting your child.

Check out www.beyondceliac.org/gluten-free-diet/overview/

It is essential to remove all traces of gluten as even a crumb may cause inflammation. This means you should use a separate toaster and segregate food preparation of gluten and non-gluten items. Tips from Coeliac UK include:

- Keep cooking utensils separate during food preparation and cooking
- Avoid frying food in the same oil that has previously been used to cook foods which contain gluten
- Use a clean grill and separate toaster or toaster bags to make gluten-free toast
- Use different breadboards and wash surfaces thoroughly
- Use separate condiments like jam, butter, mustard and mayonnaise

You can find out more from your national coeliac society.

I cried when I heard Harry had to be gluten-free. Making dietary changes is a challenge. I asked friends who knew about gluten-free eating what I should avoid. Once I became familiar with the requirements, I found it to be very manageable. Eating out does require planning ahead. Not all countries are as good as New Zealand, where menus often have a 'gf' symbol next to dishes that are suitable. It may pay to call ahead and check with the restaurant what gluten-free food they can offer. When Harry was younger and attending children's birthday parties, I gave him a party bag with gluten-free cake and treats to take with him so he wouldn't miss out.

Gluten sensitivity is a bona fide condition, distinct from coeliac disease, with its own intestinal response to gluten.

If gluten is an issue for your child and you choose to ignore it, be aware it may lead to serious health conditions later in life including a higher risk of bowel cancer.

Because we'd already removed gluten and had seen an enormous improvement in Harry's nappies and disposition, we weren't prepared to re-introduce it for the three to six months required for an accurate gut biopsy. So, although Harry has the coeliac gene, he isn't officially diagnosed as coeliac. However, if he is inadvertently exposed to gluten, he gets a sore tummy and diarrhoea.

An additional benefit of Harry going gluten-free was that

we were able to toilet train him and at last say goodbye to nappies – finally, some dollars flowing back into our pockets. Of course, we now had to spend them on expensive gluten-free food.

Lactose Intolerance

Harry was already on goat's milk when he went gluten-free, but I have read in the initial weeks on a gluten-free diet it is wise to remove cow's milk. This lowers the lactose sugar intake and allows the bowel lining time to heal. A small percentage of coeliacs remain lactose intolerant, but Harry now tolerates cow's milk and drinks it daily. He certainly hasn't suffered from stunted growth due to these health challenges. He is now 193 cm (6 feet 4 inches) tall.

General Dietary Changes

I know dietary and lifestyle modifications can reduce the impact of learning challenges because I've seen the difference they have made to Harry. However, I appreciate not everyone is interested in supplements. If this is you, feel free to skip forward to another topic. I'm sorry this section on health has been so long, and there's a lot to absorb. There are a few more things I'd like to bring to your attention. Having never seen anyone link dyslexia and health problems before, I find the topic fascinating, but before we go on, perhaps now would be a good time for you to grab a cuppa.

Dr Amen's book, Healing ADD, suggests people take a 100% multivitamin and mineral supplement and high-quality fish oil daily. I will say more about the benefits of fish oil in a moment. He also encourages people to eat a high protein and lower simple carbohydrate diet. One of his more challenging recommendations is getting kids off devices and out exercising for 30-45 minutes every day.

My Issues with Gluten

Back in the 70s and 80s, no one talked about lactose or gluten. As a child, I felt bloated after eating bread products and had a protruding belly. A doctor told me I had critically low levels of iron and I was prescribed a course of iron tablets, but no one thought to question why I was so severely anaemic. Back then, no one linked health and nutrition.

It wasn't until I was in my late thirties, when I had a back injury that wouldn't heal, that I discovered gluten could cause more problems than bowel issues. I picked up a leaflet on gluten intolerance and found joint pain and swelling are also symptoms. I removed gluten from my diet, and within two weeks, my back pain disappeared. I also felt more alert and had fewer problems with my skin.

There are two schools of thought on why gluten may cause back pain. In my case, I suspect it was a combination:

- Inflammation in the bowel forces the colon against the spine causing pain.
- Gluten causes swelling in the spinal discs which, as my disc was ruptured, prevented the fissure from healing.

I have been tested for the coeliac gene and, as I don't have it, I suspect my issue is gluten sensitivity. People have accused me of wanting to be trendy. They say because I don't have coeliac disease, I don't really need to be gluten-free. However, doctors now recognise that gluten can severely affect non-coeliacs. Scientists from the Center for Celiac Research and Treatment have found that gluten sensitivity is a bona fide condition, distinct from coeliac disease, with its own intestinal response to gluten. Although gluten-sensitive patients suffer symptoms similar to coeliac disease, they do not have the intestinal inflammation, flattening of the absorbing villi or long-term damage to the small intestine that characterises untreated coeliac disease.

About 6% of the US population have gluten sensitivity, according to the Center for Celiac Research and Treatment, compared to 1% (of the general population) who have celiac disease.[51] My reaction to gluten is just as sensitive as Harry's and maintaining a gluten-free diet is essential to my health.

www.glutenfreeliving.com/gluten-free/gluten-sensitivity/
what-is-gluten-sensitivity/

Adult Indicators of Coeliac Disease and Gluten Sensitivity

Here are some of the symptoms of gluten sensitivity that may present in adults:

- Feeling tired or exhausted and lacking energy
- Having low iron levels
- Suffering from irritable bowel, diarrhoea/constipation
- Suffering from gastric reflux, heartburn
- Feeling moody, irritable or depressed
- Bothered by headaches and migraine
- Joint aches or back pain

If like me, you are diagnosed later in life, you may well develop other autoimmune diseases (there are more than eighty to pick from). Reading the full list could cause you sleepless nights, so best not to dwell on it. Here are the top ones: Type 1 diabetes, rheumatoid arthritis, psoriasis, multiple sclerosis, lupus, Crohn's disease, ulcerative colitis, Addison's disease, Graves' disease, Sjögren's syndrome, Hashimoto's thyroiditis, Myasthenia gravis, autoimmune vasculitis and pernicious anaemia.

Iron Deficiency

As mentioned above, I was anaemic as a teenager and probably had been throughout my childhood. I suspect this was because my damaged gut could not absorb iron. Iron is essential for a healthy immune system, and I wonder if Harry's early frequent colds and sore legs were also due to his inability to absorb iron. Healing his gut has resolved these issues. If you are concerned your child may be anaemic, your doctor can request a blood test to assess iron stores and give a full iron count.

Fatty Acid Deficiency

I stumbled across the benefits of taking fish oil back in 2007 when I began taking capsules and gave Harry a liquid form of fish oil. His ADD wasn't under control, so it was difficult to assess whether the fish oil made any difference to him. However, in 2013, when Harry was eight years old, we were able to get him onto a clinical trial investigating the use of micronutrients for controlling ADD. To participate, he had to stop taking the fish oil. Within two weeks we saw a dramatic deterioration in his ability to concentrate. Once the trial was over, we put him straight back onto the fish oil. We use *Equazen* because it claims to be a brain formulation, but if you use another brand make sure it is higher EPA than DHA. "What the heck?" I hear you ask. Here is the explanation which is taken from www.equazen.co.uk/role-of-fatty-acids

"Omega-3 fatty acids are known as 'essential fatty acids' because they cannot be produced by the body, so they have to be obtained from our diet. Omega-3 fatty acids are made up of two key acids – eicosapentaenoic acid, known as EPA and docosahexaenoic acid, known as DHA. Together with omega-6 fatty acids, they are known as 'good fats'."

In case you are interested, the terms mean:

EPA (Eicosapentaenoic Acid) = Functional fatty acid

DHA (Docosahexaenoic Acid) = Structural fatty acid

The Dyslexia Research Institute has identified chromosome 18 plays a part in dyslexia and this chromosome is also implicated in an inability to metabolise fatty acids.

"Like many genes it (chromosome 18) is involved in a large number of seemingly different functions: pigmentation, reactions to stress, energy balance and obesity and possibly in the metabolism of omega 3 fatty acids. This allele may make dyslexics particularly vulnerable to dietary deficiency of omega 3 fatty acids that are found only in fish oils. Remarkably therefore, simply consuming more fish oil can often help children to greatly improve their reading, probably because this makes their magnocellular neurons work better."

A study looked at the link between fatty acid deficiency and severity of dyslexia and found that boys, in particular, showed higher levels of dyslexia if they were low in fatty acids.[52]

The Dyslexia Research Trust (DRT) has produced interesting research on this topic.

"The DRT has financed many studies that have shown that children with dyslexia, developmental coordination disorder (dyspraxia) or attention deficit hyperactivity disorder (ADHD) or combinations of these can often benefit from taking fish oil supplements. These provide the long chain polyunsaturated fatty acids (LCPUFAs) that make up 20% of the weight of the brain. The omega-3 FAs, eicosapentanoic acid (EPA) and docosahexanoic acid (DHA), can only be obtained easily from oily fish; but they are particularly essential for sharp brain function because magnocellular neurons are especially vulnerable to PUFA deficiency.
However, most people eat far too little oily fish nowadays. Our recent Oxford-Durham study showed in a double-blind randomised control trial (RCT), that 3 months'

supplemental fish oil capsules helped the reading, spelling and concentration of children with dyspraxia; their reading age improved by a massive 9 months in the 3 months."

www.dyslexic.org.uk/research/can-fish-oils-omega-3s-help-dyslexia

Fatty acids play an important role in many bodily processes, including inflammation, heart health, and brain function, and are essential in building cell membranes throughout the body and the brain.

If you want to look at other brain research about the benefits of omega-3, here's a link.

www.ncbi.nlm.nih.gov/pmc/articles/PMC3257637/

As an aside, fatty acid deficiency has also been connected to anorexia, phobias, bedwetting, abdominal complaints, compulsions and mood disturbances. I have mentioned this to several friends who have vegan children. They noticed their kids became more anxious on a vegan diet. These essential fatty acids can only be obtained from food. The Vegan Society website acknowledges that long-chain omega-3 fat (EPA and DHA) is not available from a vegan diet and supplementation may be required. www.vegansociety.com/resources/nutrition-and-health/nutrients/omega-3-and-omega-6-fats

I was vegetarian throughout my twenties, and I believe

because of my autoimmune issues, this diet damaged my health. I came across an interesting case on the web of someone overcoming her autoimmune disease by dietary intervention. Dr Terry Wahls managed to reverse her multiple sclerosis, which had left her wheelchair-bound, by abandoning her vegetarian diet and eating for brain health. Her story is a compelling case for the link between diet and autoimmune health.[53]

The Dyslexia Research Institute has identified chromosome 18 plays a part in dyslexia and this chromosome is also implicated in an inability to metabolise fatty acids.

Sugar Issues

Yup, I've joined the anti-sugar bandwagon. I know from experience Harry can't focus if he has had too much sugar. What you may not be aware of is that carbohydrates such as breakfast cereals break down into sugar. I have found giving Harry a high protein breakfast consisting of eggs or bacon or sausages (or all three now that he's a teenager) helps him be more alert. Fruit juice is also a hidden source of sugar, and a glass of milk serves him better.

For more on sugar see
www.additudemag.com/adhd-diet-nutrition-sugar/

Zinc Deficiency

Foods rich in the mineral zinc may improve the concentration of children with dyslexia. I'm no longer a vegetarian, but I was between the ages of eighteen and twenty-seven. I've since read that vegetarians need 50% more zinc than non-vegetarians. It's a wonder I could function at all back then. Poor absorption of vitamins and minerals may put a vegetarian at risk of health issues over time.

Try eating roast beef, pumpkin seeds, lamb and crab. Any type of meat or seafood should supply adequate amounts of zinc. Brazil nuts are a good source of zinc. I eat three of these per day.

Harry doesn't need to worry about his zinc levels as he takes *Hardy's Daily Essential Nutrients* to control his ADD. He was a participant on Professor Julia Rucklidge's 2014 trial into the role of micronutrients for the control of ADHD.[54] The pills Harry takes contain all the vitamins and minerals the body requires and have successfully controlled his ADD for the past eight years without the need for stimulant medication. www.try.hardynutritionals.com

Addictions

In 1992 a study of 82 randomly selected individuals in a drug rehabilitation centre astonishingly found that 80 of them (98%) were dyslexic, and 71 of these (89%) had attention deficit disorder.[55] High rates of other learning disabilities also were seen.

While all the 80 dyslexic individuals in their study had experienced difficulty in school, the research found that only six had been identified as learning disabled or placed in learning support programmes.

In addition to learning disabilities, the research found that most of their subjects also had strong family histories of biochemical, metabolic, or immune disorders. In addition, 82% of the subjects suffered from allergies or immunological problems. The data clearly showed:

"...problems relating to allergies, language, and attention deficit disorder were present from birth in a significant number and could have been utilized to predict a high risk for learning problems in school and predict susceptibility to chemical dependency or addictions."

The researchers say their study adds to evidence that "dyslexia, ADD, and chemical dependency are not simply psychological or behavioral problems but have a physiological basis."

I want to repeat that statistic – 98% of the people in the drug rehabilitation centre had dyslexia!

Sorry, DIANE, I know that sounds depressing, but being forewarned is to be forearmed. I believe Harry has an addictive personality. He fixates on hobbies, be it skateboarding or mountain biking, to the exclusion of everything else.

I have no doubt that many negative factors about living with dyslexia and finding school difficult led those people to become dependent on drugs. This is yet another reason why we must be our child's greatest cheerleader.

Singer Ozzy Osbourne said in an interview that he blames his alcohol addiction on his dyslexia. He told English newspaper *The Daily Telegraph:*[56]

> "I've always been in fear, always blamed myself for situations that have got nothing to do with me. You wake up every day and think, 'Why am I feeling like this?' I'd be afraid because I didn't feel afraid. Alcohol made it temporarily go away, but, as time went on, the fear was breaking through the alcohol. By then I couldn't put the alcohol down.[56]"

I appreciate not everyone with dyslexia has ADD, but around 30% do. Dr Amen in *Healing ADD*[34] says:

> "Type 1 ADD is likely caused by a relative deficiency of the neurotransmitter dopamine."

Dr. Nora Volkow, the director of the National Institute on Drug Abuse, says that:

"the way a brain becomes addicted to a drug is related to how a drug increases levels of the naturally-occurring neurotransmitter dopamine, which modulates the brain's ability to perceive reward reinforcement... Dopamine is what conditions us to do the things we need to do.

Using addictive drugs floods the limbic brain with dopamine – taking it up to as much as five or 10 times the normal level. With these levels elevated, the user's brain begins to associate the drug with an outsize neurochemical reward. Over time, by artificially raising the amount of dopamine our brains think is 'normal', the drugs create a need that only they can meet.[57]"

People get dopamine hits from excessive use of social media, computer games, sex, gambling, alcohol, drugs and risky sports.

Harry is only fourteen, so the jury is still out as to whether he can make it through his teen years without a drug or alcohol habit. Looking for ways to get healthy hits of dopamine, I found the following list.

www.healthline.com/nutrition/how-to-increase-dopamine#section9

- Eat a high protein diet
- Take probiotics
- Exercise regularly
- Get enough sleep

- Listen to music
- Meditate
- Take appropriate supplements
- Get enough sunlight

Harry is a happy boy when he's been out mountain biking. I call biking his passion rather than his addiction, as this keeps it positive. I'm going to encourage this sport, along with his other interests, in the hope these will give him the healthy dopamine fix he craves.

Top Fact 8

Children with dyslexia may also have specific health challenges such as issues with gluten and fatty acid deficiency. They may also be more susceptible to struggling with addictions.

Top Tip 8

If you recognise any of these health conditions in your child, consider talking to a health professional and request some blood tests. An elimination diet will help identify if gluten or dairy are problems. Add fish oil to your child's diet and investigate what other supplements may be beneficial.

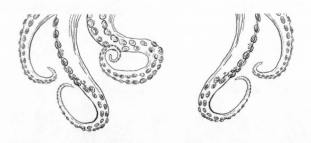

Chapter Five

How dyslexia stole Christmas (and joy in general)

The Social Effects of Dyslexia

British sitcoms of the 1970s and '80s speak volumes about society back then. One popular programme, *Some Mothers Do `Ave `Em* starred Michael Crawford as the accident-prone Frank Spencer, a man who struggled to cope with life. My family sat together on our crocheted (who would have guessed there was a 't' in that word?) throw on the sofa, laughing at Frank's inability to read social situations. Then there was *The Benny Hill Show,* filled with dirty old men chasing young women – hilarious unless you happened to be a dyslexic girl only too familiar with such lewd behaviour.

Dr Michael Ryan, a psychologist in the US who specialises

in working with learning-disabled people, has produced an excellent report on the social and emotional problems related to dyslexia and I base some of the following on his work.[58]

Shame

Guilt is easy to fix. If you feel guilty, you can attempt to put whatever you have done right, say sorry, and move on. Shame is feeling bad about **who** you are. It's much more challenging to remove these feelings.

The other day in a TEDx talk, I heard dyslexic author, Ben Foss, compare a dyslexic child to a caterpillar. I really like that simile. I want to expand upon it and say dyslexic kids are like monarch butterfly caterpillars. Have you ever seen one of these lovely creatures? As with all caterpillars, they love to eat. The trouble is, they only eat swan plants. They need to munch through a tremendous number of these before they pupate.

Monarch butterflies go places – they cross the globe. However, 90% of caterpillars fail to find enough swan plants, or are picked off by predators, before they can transform.

For the dyslexic child, their swan plant is encouragement. For them to succeed, they need a cheerleader to:

• Encourage their every step
• Help to pick them up when they fail yet again

- Point them toward activities where they can demonstrate competence
- Shower them with unconditional love

Why? Because dyslexic kids are super-sensitive. Just like those squishy little caterpillars, they are easily crushed. Verbal and physical assaults in the schoolyard, coupled with the condemnation of ignorant family members and educators, can be disastrous. For many, they will never get the chance to become the butterfly they were created to be. Instead, they remain in their cocoon of shame.

Shame dogged my early years. As a coping mechanism, I became a perfectionist. In striving never to make a mistake, my health took a huge hit. It has taken almost half a century for me to accept that I can't measure myself against others and anyway, there are no perfect people.

It's tough that dyslexic issues come to the fore just as a child is trying to work out who they are. Children between the ages of six and sixteen ask themselves, *Am I lovable, capable, competent?* Michael Ryan, in his article about social and emotional problems related to dyslexia, states that:

> "Research suggests that these feelings of inferiority develop by the age of 10. After this age, it becomes extremely difficult to help a child develop a positive self-image. This is a powerful argument for early intervention.[58]"

DIANE, I want to point out he said *extremely difficult,* not impossible. There is always hope. It may take longer to turn the situation around if the child is older, but it is still possible.

Embarrassment

Embarrassment stalks a dyslexic like a horror movie villain. It pounces in the raised eyebrows when somebody observes your handwriting, or in the comment a classmate makes about your basic spelling mistake. I may not be able to remember the product of 8x6, but I sure as hell haven't forgotten one single embarrassing moment. I, like most people with dyslexia, have shoved tonnes of embarrassing memories under my mental mattress.

One evening, when I was working at a further education college, I had to post out a mass mailing for an upcoming event. I had hundreds of envelopes to hand address (yup, I'm that old – this was *way* before mail merge). A colleague from the motor vehicle department saw me working late. Looking back, I now appreciate he was chatting me up, but I was naive, so I asked for his help. He didn't want to write addresses, but I pressed him and reluctantly he wrote one envelope. I saw he was unable to write legibly. I was embarrassed for him as he made his excuses and fled.

Dr Michael Ryan points out,

"If children meet failure and frustration, they learn that

they are inferior to others and that their efforts make very little difference. Instead of feeling powerful and productive, they learn that their environment acts upon them. They feel powerless and incompetent.[58]"

Dyslexics are often described as big picture people, which roughly translates as 'we're rubbish at detail'. Not knowing I had dyslexia caused problems when I was a designer. I really needed someone to double-check my work because I occasionally (okay, make that frequently) produced leaflets containing minor errors. Once I had thousands of copies of a large brochure printed in German, only to find that a whole paragraph had been accidentally duplicated in the typesetting and I hadn't spotted it on the proofs. I had to arrange to have stickers put over the offending paragraph – not a great design feature. The problem is that a person with dyslexia simply can't spot typos. Proofreading is a near impossibility. These days there are some great online spell-checking programmes, which certainly make my life easier.

I attended a Writers' Festival in Christchurch and heard the Australian Children's Laureate 2014–2015, Jackie French, talk about her dyslexia. Jackie has written over 140 books and is unabashed about the fact that she can't spell. Her website says that she:

"wrote her first children's book 'Rain Stones' in a desperate attempt to earn $106.40 to register her car while living in a shed with a wallaby called Fred, a black snake called Gladys and a wombat called Smudge. The editor at HarperCollins said it was the messiest, worst spelt manuscript they'd ever received. The mess was because Smudge the wombat left his droppings on the typewriter every night. The spelling was because Jackie is dyslexic. Jackie recommends all beginning writers misspell their first book, so it stands out of the pile."

Being unembarrassed to declare in public that she has dyslexia has made Jackie French confident in her abilities. She's a great storyteller. Her books have sold millions of copies and won over 60 awards. She didn't let her spelling mistakes stop her from becoming a world-class author. Jackie's talk inspired me that day.

Low Self-esteem, Anxiety and Depression

Neurologist Samuel Orton was one of the first people to document the emotional aspects of dyslexia. He noticed that most children with dyslexia are happy and well-adjusted until they hit difficulties with learning to read and write. In time their frustration mounts as their classmates and siblings overtake them.

Clinical psychologist Michael Ryan found that 20% of people with dyslexia suffer from depression and another 20% suffer from an anxiety disorder.[59]

He states:

"Dyslexics' frustration often centres on their inability to meet expectations… this is particularly true of those who develop perfectionist expectations in order to deal with their anxiety. They grow up believing that it is 'terrible' to make a mistake. However, their learning disability, almost by definition, means that these children will make many 'careless' or 'stupid' mistakes. This is extremely frustrating to them, as it makes them feel chronically inadequate."

The knock to self-esteem that occurs when a child fails to read cannot be underestimated. Self-esteem is best understood as the discrepancy between the 'ideal self' and the 'self-image.'[60] The problem a dyslexic child faces is their repeated failures mean they see themselves as far from their 'ideal self'. As Michael Ryan puts it:

"Anxiety is the most frequent emotional symptom reported by dyslexic adults. Dyslexics feel fearful because of their constant frustration and confusion in school. These feelings are exacerbated by the inconsistencies of dyslexia. Because they cannot anticipate failure, entering new situations becomes anxiety-provoking. Anxiety causes humans to avoid whatever frightens them… many teachers and parents misinterpret this avoidance as laziness. In fact, the dyslexic's hesitancy to participate in school activities such as homework is related more to anxiety and confusion than to apathy. Social scientists have frequently observed that frustration produces anger. This can be clearly seen in many dyslexics.[59]"

Having dyslexia means you never know when you're going to slip up and make a fool of yourself. You are always in a state of anxiety, which leads to frustration and outbursts of anger. Sometimes, as in dyslexic lead singer of The Prodigy, Keith Flint's case, this outpouring of anger is evident for the entire world to see. Often the violence is self-directed and may lead to self-harm.

I am not surprised, having read Dr Michael Ryan's work, that Harry suffers from low mood and poor self-esteem. Harry frequently calls himself stupid, which is heartbreaking for me to hear. Some children may require anti-anxiety medication and/or anti-depressants. We have found a natural remedy from Xtend-Life, which has helped both of us. Taking this supplement daily, in conjunction with healthy nutrition, enough sleep and plenty of exercise, balances our mood.

20% of people with dyslexia suffer from depression and another 20% suffer from an anxiety disorder.

Anxiety is a natural state for many people with dyslexia. Having to stand up in front of the class and give a speech, even when he has a wonderful talk prepared, turns Harry into a gibbering wreck. His heightened levels of anxiety are typically based on specific events.

Persistent anxiety, however, is not based on one-off events. In a child, this may look like the following:

- Trouble falling asleep
- Fear of being alone
- Picking at skin
- Nail biting
- Strong startle response
- Being overly self-critical
- OCD-like behaviours (e.g. checking and rechecking the door to make sure it is locked or being obsessive about arranging objects 'just so')
- Suddenly avoiding social contact
- Frequent urination

If you recognise your child in the above list, you may need to talk to a doctor about trialling anti-anxiety medication or consider trying a natural anti-anxiety supplement such as the one previously mentioned. For a full rundown on anxiety, check out this page on. www.additudemag.com/anxiety-disorders-in-children-symptoms/

Learning some mindfulness techniques has also helped Harry. He knows how to take slow deep belly breaths and focus on his breathing. This has proved useful when he finds it difficult getting to sleep, and he listens to mindfulness 'body scan' relaxations on YouTube when he's particularly stressed.

The Effect on the Family of Having a Child with Dyslexia

In Gayle Zieman, PhD's article, 'How Families Cope with Their Dyslexic Child', on dyslexiadx.com/articles-cope. php, Gayle makes the excellent point that "dyslexia isn't just an academic and individual problem; it's also a family problem." Harry having dyslexia has had an impact on his sister, and on our parenting style. What works for a child without dyslexia may not work for one with it. This apparent unfairness has caused trouble in our household. Harry is quick to point out anything which looks like special treatment for his sister, be that the age she got her first phone or the time she goes to bed. We treat each child as an individual. To ensure our daughter feels loved and appreciated, we try our best to take an interest in her and her activities. Despite this, I know she would say Harry gets more of our attention.

"Dyslexia isn't just an academic and individual problem; it's also a family problem."

Gayle Zieman

Harry's homework is often a family affair. My husband and I were proud when Harry's maths project did well; we had all helped him. We can joke about it because we are just aiming to get him through school. No doubt Harry will thrive once he leaves and can follow his passions. Until then, we are resigned to spending however long it takes to help him with his homework.

An Inability to Identify and Name Feelings

Harry, like many people with dyslexia, struggles to separate out his feelings. He can have a fabulous day at school until the last lesson. If the teacher shouts, or he gets into trouble at that point, he will come home raging about how terrible his day was. When we talk it through, I discover that only one thing upset him.

In Jane McWilliams' thesis, *Dyslexia and Intimate Relationships*,[61] one man with dyslexia explained this phenomenon as follows:

"I don't have any feelings. I only have one… I'm either all happy, I'm all sad, or I'm all hungry." He also said, "I can't talk about my feelings… I don't like talking about those."

I have found Harry to be very similar. Allowing time for him to listen to his favourite music when he is flooded by emotion helps calm him. Another essential consideration is hunger. As a teenage boy, Harry is hungry 99% of the time. Making sure he has regular snacks is important. When he was five years old, he had a lovely teacher who understood this. She asked him to have a snack before he attempted anything complicated. To this day, he has a pot of nuts in his lunch box for this very purpose.

Vulnerability to Abuse

DIANE, you may feel the following section does not apply to your child. I don't want to scare you, but there is statistical evidence that children with learning difficulties such as dyslexia are more vulnerable to abuse. I'm including this tricky topic because I want to offer suggestions on how to keep your child safe.

A University of Toronto research paper, 'The Association Between Childhood Physical Abuse and Dyslexia: Findings from a Population-Based Study' found that 35% of adults with dyslexia reported they were physically abused before they turned eighteen. In contrast, 7% of the general population reported that they had experienced physical abuse.

In 1992 the British Medical Journal under the heading, 'Another Iceberg', looked at the link between sexual abuse and learning disabilities and stated that "American studies suggest that between one in three and one in four teenagers and young adults with learning difficulties have suffered sexual abuse.[62]" The general population risk for sexual abuse is one in ten. Emotional immaturity puts dyslexics at a disadvantage, making them easy prey for perverts.

"American studies suggest that between one in three and one in four teenagers and young adults with learning difficulties have suffered sexual abuse." [62]

I had several instances in my childhood and teens where my naivety put me at risk. I loved to draw, and one day, when I was eleven years old, I went down to the local museum to sketch the stuffed animals. The building was deserted. I sat at a glass case drawing a fawn, and a museum worker approached and struck up a conversation. A little bit of background would be useful at this point. I am the daughter of a teacher and a policeman. I'm sure they had warned me not to talk to strangers but, in that context, I didn't see this man, who was wearing a museum uniform, as a stranger. The man told me the best animals were kept in the storeroom and I should go with him, which I merrily did. I had a quick look around and said I wanted to finish drawing the deer and went back out. Looking back, I had a lucky escape. I suspect after a short conversation he picked that I was a suitable target and thought it was worth trying his luck.

One of the most important ways to protect your child is to stay well connected to what they are doing, know where they are going, and with whom they are spending time. This digital age throws up even more potential for harm. A friend of mine was horrified to discover her dyslexic daughter was being groomed online by a paedophile posing as a teen. The family was going through a tough time with their other child who had cancer. Their loss of connection with their dyslexic daughter inadvertently put her at risk. Fortunately, the police caught the man before harm was done.

According to the US Department of Justice (nsopw.gov), only 10% of perpetrators were strangers to the child they abused, and more worrying still, 23% of the perpetrators were themselves children.

10 ways to protect your child against sexual abuse

The following is used with permission and is abridged from the Child Mind Institute (childmind.org). It first appeared on Natasha Daniel's website, Anxious Toddlers.

1. **Talk about body parts early with your child.**
   Name body parts very early and feel comfortable using the correct words so a child can talk clearly if something inappropriate happens.

2. **Teach them about parts of the body that are private.**
   Explain that Mummy, Daddy and the doctor are the only people who should see them with their clothes off.

3. **Teach your child body boundaries.**
   Tell your child no one should touch their private parts and that they shouldn't touch someone else's private parts. This second part is important because sexual

abuse often begins with a perpetrator asking the child to touch them or someone else.

4. **Tell your child body secrets are not okay.**
Most perpetrators ask the child to keep the abuse secret. It may be done in a friendly way such as, "If you tell, we won't be able to see each other again," or it may be a threat. Explain to your child body secrets are not okay, and they should always tell you if someone tries to make them keep a body secret.

5. **Tell them no one should take pictures of their private parts.**
This is often missed by parents, but there is a whole sick world of paedophiles who love to take and trade pictures of naked children online.

6. **Teach your child how to get out of scary or uncomfortable situations.**
Some children are uncomfortable saying 'no' to an older person. Explain it is okay to tell an adult they must leave if something feels wrong. Tell them they can always say they need to go to the bathroom and leave the situation.

7. **Have a code word your children can use when they feel unsafe or want to be picked up.**
As children get older, give them a code word they can use if they feel unsafe when they are a guest at another house.

8. **Tell your child they will never be in trouble if they tell you a body secret.**

    Children often say they didn't tell anyone because they thought they would get into trouble. This fear is commonly used by the perpetrator.

9. **Tell your child a body touch might tickle or feel good.**

    Many parents talk about 'good and bad touch', but this can be confusing as these touches may not hurt or feel bad. The term 'secret touch' is more appropriate.

10. **Tell your child that these rules apply even with people they know or with other children.**

    Young children often think of a bad guy as a cartoonish villain. It is important to say something like, "Mummy and Daddy might touch your private parts when we are cleaning you – but no one else should touch you there. Not friends, not aunts or uncles, not teacher or coaches. Even if you like them, or think they are in charge, they should still not touch your private parts."

Find natural times to mention this information, such as at bath times or when they are running about in the house naked. A one-off conversation is not enough for a child with dyslexia. Repetition of the information is essential, but there is no need to frighten the child, so keep the conversation light and matter of fact.

Other ways to keep your child safe:

- Choose caregivers carefully. Get and check references for babysitters and afterschool carers and occasionally drop in unannounced. Be aware that sex offences are also committed by women.
- Make it clear to any carer that you don't want your child left in someone else's care without your permission.
- Always make sure there is more than one adult in charge of a large group of children and offer to go with your child on organised activities to get to know the people in charge.
- Pay special attention to friendships involving older children and ask what games they play or movies they watch together.

Bullying

Steven Spielberg struggled at school but was only diagnosed with dyslexia as an adult. In an interview, he revealed he was a target for school bullies. What helped him overcome his difficulties was discovering his love of filmmaking.

Bullyingfree.nz has this to say about what constitutes bullying:

"Whether bullying is physical, verbal, or social (relational), four widely accepted factors can be used to identify it:

- Bullying is deliberate – harming another person intentionally
- Bullying involves a misuse of power in a relationship
- Bullying is usually not a one-off – it is repeated or has the potential to be repeated over time
- Bullying involves behaviour that can cause harm – it is not a normal part of growing up"

Other students may mock a child who has dyslexia for their inability to read and write at the same level as their peers. This can lead to bullying in the playground. Making sure your child understands that dyslexia is not a sign of low intelligence may help them bounce back from such playground taunts.

Dyslexics can be emotionally several years behind their peers, which makes developing friendships in school a struggle. We kept Harry back slightly at the beginning of primary school, and I have no doubt it was for the best. The way his birthday fell, meant he could have been a year ahead. After only six months of Year 0, the school put him into a blended Year 1 – 2 class. I asked for him to be dropped back to repeat the first year. His lack of emotional maturity would have caused him to struggle if he had remained at the higher level.

Harry finds it difficult to discern when children are being sneaky or manipulative. Older children have asked him to buy them sweets or give them his possessions in return for their friendship. For Harry, alpha males in any group can cause him problems. Alpha males look to assert dominance. When I Googled 'alpha male,' I found numerous sites saying to be an alpha male was to be 'a real man'. Alpha males enjoy competing, teasing, verbal provocations and banter. They are looking to discover who they can boss around. Sadly, at the bottom of the pecking order comes the kid who is unable to respond quickly to verbal assaults due to auditory processing difficulties, or who shows a sensitive nature.

There are plenty of sites online, and numerous books you can read, about beating bullying. Just Google, 'How to bully-proof your child'. Staying emotionally close and involved in your child's life is vital. Knowing when something is upsetting your child and being willing to teach coping strategies or intervene if bullying is severe, is essential.

Some say bullying is worse today, but when I was at school, bullies were also drawn to me. I avoided the playground and hung out in the library at lunchtime. Whenever I did try to join in with the 'cool' kids, I usually ended up in trouble. I can see similar issues in Harry. He likes energetic boys, yet he is often crushed by their cruel comments. It's as if people with dyslexia have thinner skin and a light above their heads which draws bullies to them like moths to a flame. Harry certainly has a sensitive nature. He finds it difficult to understand why children choose to be mean. He could be described as naive or gullible. I'm reminded of my younger self when I see him struggling.

A few years ago, Lord Robert Winston made a television series called *Child of our Time*. In it, he analysed the factors that helped a child to succeed in school. Surprisingly, one of his top tips was to make sure your child does not look like the odd one out. When I started high school, my mother bought me a blue vinyl shopping bag. It was the most uncool school bag ever! I eventually had to cut the handles with scissors because the thing refused to wear out. Not allowing me to have a 'normal' schoolbag was tantamount to attaching a 'kick me' notice to my back. I appreciate you may not be able to keep up with all the latest fashions for your child, (who can?), but ensuring they aren't regarded as 'uncool' is one way to help them avoid the attention of school bullies.

Dyslexics can be emotionally several years behind their peers, which makes developing friendships in school a struggle.

Cyberbullying

When I was a kid, I was kicked down the stairs at school and pushed under in the swimming pool, but at least I got a respite from school bullies when I was at home. With the advent of smartphones, this escape is no longer assured.

Online, people are often judged by the content and quality

of their messages and posts. If errors slip through, a dyslexic child may appear unintelligent even when they use auto-correct programmes. So-called 'friends' may mock your child's inability to spell basic words. Harry now uses speech-to-text for all his messaging. He talks into his phone and the message either goes as a voice text or it is converted into text. This is quicker for him, and it also side-steps spelling.

According to Cyberbullying statistics from the i-SAFE foundation:

- Over half of adolescents and teens have been bullied online, and about the same number have engaged in cyberbullying.
- Over 25% of adolescents and teens have been bullied repeatedly through their cell phones or the internet.
- Well over half of young people do not tell their parents when cyberbullying occurs.

www.bullyingstatistics.org/content/cyber-bullying-statistics.html

Harry has a smartphone. I'm very aware that although he is fourteen, he operates at a much lower emotional level. It is common for children with dyslexia to be cyberbullied, and therefore Harry didn't have a phone until he went to high school. It is important to monitor what social media your child is using and to watch out for behavioural changes, which may indicate bullying.

Self-harm and Suicide

If your child is in primary school, you may wonder why I'm mentioning this topic, but it's because I believe it's better to be forearmed than to stick your head in the sand. Feel free to skip this section if you don't think it is relevant.

A recent study in Canada found there was a higher risk of suicide attempts for people with learning disabilities.[63]

The report authors speculate that high rates of sexual and physical abuse in this population may be to blame. The lead author, Professor Esme Fuller-Thomson, noted:

"Learning disabilities such as dyslexia cast a very long shadow...our findings of the strong link between learning disabilities and suicide attempts provide an additional reason to prioritize the early detection and timely provision of effective educational interventions for children with dyslexia and other learning problems."

Prodigy musician and singer, Keith Flint, who had the chart-topping hit, 'Firestarter', bears out this statistic. Flint had dyslexia. He came from a loving family, and his teachers remember him as an intelligent but hyperactive boy. Friends recall Flint was polite and well brought up. Leaving school at fifteen, he had no qualifications and worked as a roofer. He became addicted to drugs, but eventually cleaned up his act and took up motorcycle racing as he enjoyed driving fast. Flint did not replicate the success he found on the racing track in his private life, where he struggled to maintain relationships. Sadly, at forty-nine, he took his own life.

If you spot signs of self-harm, or your child talks about suicide, it is essential to seek professional help. Your doctor should be your first port of call, however, if this is a life-threatening situation don't hesitate to call the emergency services. Your child may require help from specialist mental health professionals.

There was a higher risk of suicide attempts for women with learning disabilities (16,6%) compared to women without (3.3%). Men with learning disabilities were also more likely to attempt suicide (7.7% vs 2.1%).

The Need for Protection from Toxic People and Unhealthy Relationships

Children need to be taught who will pick on their weaknesses if exposed. I don't advocate a child telling everybody about their dyslexia. Learning the difference between safe people and unsafe people requires coaching. The website www.heysigmund.com has some good advice on keeping kids safe from toxic people. The following is abridged from a post by Karen Young.

"Toxic people can come in the form of teachers, coaches, relatives, parents (their own and the parents of others) and friends. The only thing anyone needs to be toxic is a mouth. The potential is in all of us.

Kids won't always be able to say when something doesn't feel right, particularly if it's in response to an adult whose authority they've been taught to respect or whose intentions they've been taught to trust. The first sign that something isn't right might be in their behaviour. Here are some things to watch out for. Remember, you're looking for changes from their normal:

- They seem withdrawn
- They don't want to go to somewhere they previously had no problems going (e.g. school, soccer, dancing) Remember that you're looking for changes from the norm. If your child has always had trouble saying goodbye at school drop-off that doesn't mean there is a problem, they're just anxious about leaving you
- They cry more easily than usual, or more often
- They lack energy
- They aren't as interested in things they used to enjoy
- They have unexplained tummy aches, headaches or other pains or illnesses
- They're clingy
- They're aggressive or more cranky than usual
- They seem worried more than usual
- They seem more controlling than usual (When

something feels out of control in one part of their life, a typical response is to try to take control in other areas)

- They're treating their siblings differently (They might treat younger people the way someone is treating them)"

I find sitting on Harry's bed at the end of each day is invaluable for finding out what's worrying him. Usually, just as I'm about to leave the room, he opens up about what's on his mind. I sometimes need to force myself to pause and listen when I have a million other things I want to do, but I figure these ten minutes will save me a fortune in therapy bills down the track.

People with narcissistic and sociopathic disorders target vulnerable people. Harry may attract manipulative and controlling partners because of his naivety. Lesley Elliott, mother of Sophie Elliott, who was murdered by a man with a narcissistic personality disorder, wrote the book *Loves Me Not*. In this, she explains how to stay safe in relationships.[64]

Some of her suggestions to avoid an abusive relationship are below.

- Think twice about starting a relationship with someone who can hold some sort of power and control over your life, such as a supervisor or boss.
- A significant age difference, ten years or more can leave the younger person open to abusive behaviour.
- In a healthy relationship, both parties communicate

equally. There is no one constantly texting or failing to respond to texts.

- Abusers use entitlement and threats to control a partner's behaviour.
- Sometimes abusers threaten to hurt themselves or to commit suicide to manipulate their partner.
- Name-calling, i.e. saying you're ugly, too fat etc. is psychological abuse.
- Self-centeredness is also a trait of a psychological abuser.
- Physical violence can escalate quickly. Avoid contact with someone who has physically abused you.
- Pressuring someone for sex, or using threats to get sex, are signs of an unhealthy relationship.
- If one partner spends a lot of time watching porn and insists the other person watches it when they don't want to, that is not a healthy relationship.

Research has shown that when it comes to violence in intimate relationships, men and women are both victims and perpetrators in equal amounts.[64]Although it may be difficult to intervene if your teen becomes involved in an abusive relationship, do encourage your child to seek help. If your child is still in education, the school counsellors may be able to help support you and your child.

The focus of this book is children with dyslexia. Dyslexia is an inherited condition; therefore, often one or more parent also has it. If you would like to investigate how dyslexia may

be impacting your intimate relationship, Jane McWilliams'
thesis is an excellent read.[61]

Top Fact 9

Children with dyslexia are more at risk from abuse,

bullying and self-harm.

Top Tip 9

Be aware of a dyslexic child's vulnerability to abuse.

Talk with your child about how to stay safe in both the

real and virtual world.

Chapter Six

My book about me

The Importance of Finding Strengths and Competencies

Obviously, dyslexia was not the only formative factor in making me who I am today. I was fortunate enough to find success in my artwork and was forever winning colouring and painting competitions. Having that ability got me through school and set me on a creative path.

Harry's passion is sport. He spends every spare moment kicking a football up and down the hall and scoring a goal by blasting it into my fruit bowl (grr) or riding his mountain bike down the steepest slopes he can find. I know that not all children with dyslexia can find an outlet in sport, or art for that matter, but discovering their passion will help buffer them against repeated academic failure.

Ben Foss's book, *The Dyslexia Empowerment Plan,*[26] is an excellent resource for identifying and building on your child's strengths.

Michael Ryan's paper on dyslexia-related social and emotional problems has some helpful suggestions on how to help a dyslexic child overcome their emotional issues including the following:

"During the past 25 years, I have interviewed many dyslexic adults. Some have learned to deal successfully with their learning problems, while others have not. My experiences suggest that in addition to factors such as intelligence and socio-economic status, other things affect the dyslexic's chances for success.

First, early in the child's life, someone has been extremely supportive and encouraging. Second, the young dyslexic found an area in which he or she could succeed. Finally, successful dyslexics appear to have developed a commitment to helping others.

Both teachers and parents need to offer consistent, ongoing encouragement and support. However, one rarely hears about this very important way to help youngsters.

I believe encouragement involves at least four elements. First, listening to children's feelings. Anxiety, anger and depression are daily companions for dyslexics. However, their language problems make it difficult for them to express their feelings. Therefore, adults must help them learn to talk about their feelings.

Teachers and parents must reward effort, not just 'the product'. For the dyslexic, grades should be less important than progress.

When confronting unacceptable behavior, adults must not inadvertently discourage the dyslexic child. Words such as 'lazy' or 'incorrigible' can seriously damage the child's self-image.

Finally, it is important to help students set realistic goals for themselves. Most dyslexic students set perfectionistic and unattainable goals. By helping the child set an attainable goal, teachers can change the cycle of failure.

Even more important, the child needs to recognize and rejoice in his or her successes. To do so, he or she needs to achieve success in some area of life. In some cases, the dyslexic's strengths are obvious, and many dyslexics' self-esteem has been salvaged by prowess in athletics, art, or mechanics. However, the dyslexic's strengths are often more subtle and less obvious. Parents and teachers need to find ways to relate the child's interests to the demands of real life.

Finally, many successful dyslexic adults deal with their own pain by reaching out to others. They may do volunteer work for charities or churches or choose vocations that require empathy and a social conscience. These experiences help dyslexics feel more positive about themselves and deal more effectively with their pain and frustration.

Many opportunities exist in our schools, homes and churches for dyslexics to help others. One important area is peer tutoring. If dyslexic students do well in math or science, they can be asked to tutor a classmate who is struggling." [58]

Ben Foss's book, The Dyslexia Empowerment Plan,[26] is an excellent resource for identifying and building on your child's strengths.

Success Attributes

A 20-year longitudinal study from the Frostig Center[65] followed the lives of 50 individuals with learning disabilities from childhood to adulthood, measured success by:

- Educational attainment
- Employment status
- Social relationships
- Psychological health
- Family relationships
- Independent living
- Life satisfaction

It identified the following success attributes in individuals who had succeeded in life:

Self-awareness

Both the successful group and the unsuccessful group referred to themselves as 'learning disabled', however, those in the successful group recognised that their difficulties were only one aspect of their lives and they weren't defined by their challenges. The most successful participants were able to find employment in niche areas which matched their strengths.

Proactivity

The successful individuals were active in community activities and believed they had the power to control their own destiny. Unsuccessful study participants tended to respond to events and failed to see that there were multiple solutions to every problem.

Perseverance

Both the successful and unsuccessful participants reportedly *kept going despite adversity*. But the successful group knew how to find their way around obstacles and were able to quit when necessary and try something else.

Goal Setting

The unsuccessful people in the study set goals that were vague, unrealistic or unachievable. They lacked the self-awareness to take account of their own abilities and strengths.

In contrast, the successful people identified their strengths early on, often while still at school, and set goals that were concrete, realistic and achievable. They had goals in all areas of their lives, not just for academic or career success.

Presence and Use of Effective Social Support Systems

Both groups in the study stressed how vital support was from family, teachers, therapists, co-workers.

In early adulthood, the role of mentors and significant others who gave them support, encouragement, and emotional help, and were sounding boards for reality testing, was important.

In the 20-year follow-up, the relationship between the successful informants and their 'significant others' began to change. The more successful group was able to have reciprocated relationships with their mentors and assume responsibility for their actions and lives. The less successful group was still dependent on family and were unable to live independently.

Emotional Stability

All participants said that their learning difficulties had caused them stress, with some mentioning panic attacks and depression.

Successful participants were able to recognise emotional triggers and develop coping strategies. The unsuccessful participants were 'blindsided' by emotional states which overwhelmed them. Maintaining good peer relationships and keeping socially active were two effective coping mechanisms that most clearly differentiated the successful from the unsuccessful group.

There is a book based on this study which suggests activities to develop these success attributes. *The 6 Success Factors for Children with Learning Disabilities,* by Richard D. Lavoie.[66]

Filling your Child's Emotional Tank

When I read Gary D. Chapman and Ross Campbell's book, *The 5 Love Languages of Children,*[67] it transformed the way I understood love and, being a visual thinker, their concept of an *emotional tank* resonated with me.

The following is an excerpt from their book:

"Filling the Emotional Tank

By speaking your child's own love language, you can fill his "emotional tank" with love. When your child feels loved, he is much easier to discipline and train than when his "emotional tank" is running near empty.

Every child has an emotional tank, a place of emotional strength that can fuel him through the challenging days of childhood and adolescence. Just as cars are powered by reserves in the gas tank, our children are fuelled from their emotional tanks. We must fill our children's emotional tanks for them to operate as they should and reach their potential.

But with what do we fill these tanks? Love, of course, but love of a particular kind that will enable our children to grow and function properly.

We need to fill our children's emotional tanks with un-conditional love because real love is always unconditional. Unconditional love is a love that accepts and affirms a child for who he is, not for what he does. No matter what he does (or does not do), the parent still loves him. Sadly, parents often display a love that is conditional; it depends on something other than their children just being. Conditional love is based on performance and is often associated with training techniques that offer gifts, rewards, and privileges to children who behave or perform in desired ways.

Of course, it is necessary to train and/or discipline our

children – but only after their emotional tanks have been filled. Those tanks can be filled with only one premium fuel: unconditional love. Our children have 'love tanks' ready to be filled (and refilled – they can deplete regularly). Only unconditional love can prevent problems such as resentment, feelings of being unloved, guilt, fear and insecurity. Only as we give our children unconditional love, will we be able to deeply understand them and deal with their behaviours, whether good or bad...

For a child to feel love, we must learn to speak her unique love language. Every child has a special way of perceiving love. There are basically five ways children (indeed, all people) speak and understand emotional love. They are: physical touch, words of affirmation, quality time, gifts and acts of service. If you have several children in your family, chances are they speak different languages, for just as different children have different personalities, they may hear in different love languages. Typically, two children need to be loved in different ways."

In case you skimmed through that, here are the five love languages again:

- Physical touch
- Words of affirmation
- Quality time
- Gifts
- Acts of service

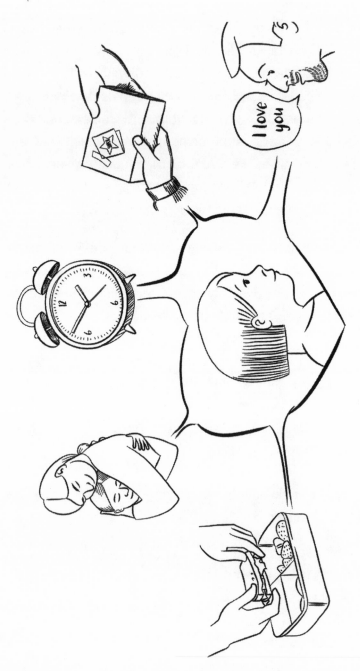

I believe this emotional tank concept is particularly helpful for dyslexic children because their academic performance is often erratic or poor. I tend to think of my son as having an *emotional colander*. I am willing to admit I often inadvertently shoot another hole in it when I roll my eyes as he misspells a word he knew last week, or patronise him when he fails to understand a simple idiom such as 'face the music'.

For Harry, the filling of his love tank involves lots of *physical touch*. He is a hugger. This does not come naturally to me; my other child's love language is gifts. However, I am learning to be a hugger and, even though he's now fourteen and is much taller than me, he sometimes needs a long hug in the morning just to get through the day.

His secondary love language is *words of affirmation*. I suspect this is the case for most people with dyslexia. There's often a loud voice inside the head of a person with dyslexia continually telling them they are *hopeless* and *stupid*. To counteract this negative onslaught, a parent needs to offer positive, affirming messages.

I admit I often forget this. Harry sometimes says, "Am I still your special treasure?" This is him asking for affirmation. Thank goodness he has learned to ask for what he needs.

Teachers and parents must reward effort, not just "the product". For the dyslexic, grades should be less important than progress.

Debriefing After School

I appreciate I'm fortunate to work from home. I'm usually in when Harry returns from school; invariably, he is exhausted. Some quiet time listening to music or watching mountain biking YouTube videos helps him unwind. I make sure he has eaten before I ask him about his day.

When he was younger, he was generally happy to chat. Now that he's a teen, I find I need to pick my moments to talk with him. Sometimes he needs to be left alone to chill. In the past, I've asked him to rate his day out of 10, with 10 being the best. This approach isn't always a good indication of how school went because Harry tends to forget what happened in the morning. If he is in the mood to speak, I try to avoid asking questions that will elicit one or two-word answers such as:

- How was school?
- Did you have fun at school?
- Who did you sit with?
- Was your teacher nice?

The sort of questions that work well are:

- What was the best thing you did today?
- What was the most interesting thing your teacher said?
- What were most of the kids doing at break time?

The Role of Intuition

People with dyslexia are very intuitive. According to psychologytoday.com, intuition is defined as:

> "The ability to know something directly without analytic reasoning, bridging the gap between conscious and nonconscious parts of our mind, and also between instinct and reason."

Learning to work with intuition has been helpful in my life. It is easy to knock the role of intuition in our rational society; logic usually trumps it. People with dyslexia have made many fascinating discoveries by following their intuition, see Chapter Seven for examples. Trusting intuition is to be encouraged.

As an adult, I have found keeping a journal first thing in the morning helpful for me to connect with my intuition. I picked this tip up from Julia Cameron's excellent book, *The Artist's Way.*

To help your child connect with their intuition, encourage them to keep a journal. They could create one with voice-to-text or as a series of mind maps. Children must allow their inner dialogue to flow without fear of ridicule, and therefore, they shouldn't show their journal to others.

The Benefits of a Spiritual Life

I wasn't brought up in a religious household; however, I became a Christian when I was seventeen years old. Finding out about a loving God who accepted me has made an enormous difference to my life. Many people with dyslexia find solace in spirituality, whether in Christianity or another faith.

Although I initially found church boring, I was attracted to the character of Jesus. He was a master storyteller who worked with his hands as a carpenter and never wrote a book. No wonder he's attractive to someone with dyslexia. One of his stories particularly appeals to me. It can be found in the New Testament of the Bible in Matthew 7 verses 24 – 27.

"The Two Builders

So then, anyone who hears these words of mine and obeys them is like a wise man who built his house on rock. The rain poured down, the rivers flooded over, and the wind blew hard against that house. But it did not fall, because it was built on rock.

But anyone who hears these words of mine and does not obey them is like a foolish man who built his house on sand. The rain poured down, the rivers flooded over, the wind blew hard against that house, and it fell. And what a terrible fall that was!" (GNT)

I have had many 'storms' in my life: divorce, infertility, earthquakes, illness and the death of family members and friends. My faith is the rock I cling to in tough times. Without it, I know I would be swept away by the trials of life.

Accepting God's unconditional love for me fills my emotional tank each day. Because of my faith, I believe I get to wipe the slate of my life clean each day, or frequently multiple times per day. That's great news for my self-esteem. I haven't forgotten my embarrassing moments, but I visualise them along with all my failures and mistakes at the bottom of the sea with a 'No Fishing' sign floating above them.

Because of God's love for me, there's no need to be burdened by my frequent 'dumb' mistakes. I have found being able to pray about problems helps me to process them. I know Harry finds being part of a Christian youth group gives him a supportive group of friends who accept him.

Sadly, my point about being vigilant for abusers and perverts also applies in the church context. The church has attracted some people who prey on vulnerable people, and the scandal of sexual abuse in the church is appalling.

Jesus cherished children and never condoned their abuse.

Millions of people find comfort in the church. I have found

strength in knowing God unconditionally loves me, and he made me the way I am for a purpose; I'm not defective. God has a good plan for my life. I don't have to be perfect because I know Jesus, who is perfect.

For more on Christianity see christianityworks.co.nz/jesus/

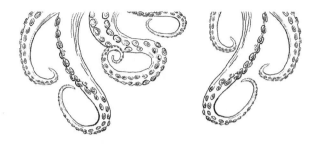

Chapter Seven

I can draw, build, design and sing

Nurturing the Talents Which Often Come with Dyslexia

Sharing stories of successful people who have overcome their dyslexia is a great way to encourage your child. I gained the confidence to start a career in writing when I discovered that Jules Verne, Agatha Christie, W.B Yeats, F. Scott Fitzgerald and John Irving, amongst others, overcame their dyslexia to become successful authors.

Your child may not be exceptionally gifted, but just seeing people who have dyslexia can do well in life will encourage them. Having hope is essential to feeling positive about life. When a child is struggling in school, hearing about people who also failed at school but went on to do amazing things may inspire hope.

In their book, *The Dyslexic Advantage,* Brock and Fernette Eide outline the talents of dyslexics that may be due to a difference in brain structure. The Eides say there are currently about twenty-five papers exploring the connection between dyslexia and certain talents and abilities. While most studies are made with small samples, and are published in obscure journals, the Eides say:

"What mattered ... was the recurrent evidence found around the world of people who struggled with dyslexia excelling in areas like engineering, the arts, design, and entrepreneurship.[68]"

The Arts

Music

The Arts are a vehicle for self-expression, and music is a field in which many people with dyslexia have excelled. Harry showed musical ability from a young age. I have videos of him as a preschooler dancing to music, playing air-guitar, and using anything and everything as a microphone. He also loves listening to music. If he's stressed or over-whelmed by his school day, he uses music to relax. As mentioned earlier, he tried piano lessons when he was younger, but they ended in disaster. One issue was he was tired, another was, at that stage, he couldn't read, and therefore following music was impossible. Over the years he's attempted to learn the recorder, ukulele and guitar all without success. I suspect this is partly because his ADD makes it difficult to persevere with things that require practice. For the last three years he's played the saxophone as part of a jazz band, and he loves it. The sax has worked for him because he can now read. I don't think he's heading for a music career, but he certainly finds it a balm to his soul.

Singer Carly Simon and her two children have dyslexia. She was reported on understood.org saying, "My family has been given the gift of music. We all take to music because music is something that we can do so much more easily than we can in the reading department."

Lou Reed, founder of the band The Velvet Underground, is also quoted on understood.org: "I've always had trouble reading anything with long paragraphs. I'm a little dyslexic, and I reverse things. I thought I was unemployable."

"My family has been given the gift of music. We all take to music because music is something that we can do so much more easily than we can in the reading department." Carly Simon

Famous Musicians

- Joss Stone – Singer
- Joe Perry and Steven Tyler – Aerosmith
- Jewel – Singer
- Chris Robinson – Black Crowes
- Noel Gallagher – Oasis
- Ozzy Osbourne – Black Sabbath
- Keith Flint – The Prodigy
- Stewart Copeland – Drummer with The Police
- Nigel Kennedy – Violinist
- Cher – Singer
- John Lennon – The Beatles

Dyslexic musicians may have problems with:

- Sight-reading music
- Remembering instructions in lessons and/or aural work

- De-coding information in music exams
- Organisation of rehearsals, taking the correct music to practice and getting to lessons on time.

The following ten tips for dyslexia-friendly music teaching are used with permission and are from the British Dyslexia Association website.[69]

1. Be imaginative and patient. Think outside of the box!

2. **One size doesn't fit all:** everyone is different. How do you/does your student learn best? The **student** should choose what works best for him or her. **Don't impose ideas.**

3. **Structure** all activities: chunk information; build it up.

4. Use **multi-sensory** approaches: hear; see; feel; read; write; move around; hands on... Use **colour** (of the student's choice) for highlighting etc.

5. Use **over-learning**/revision/embedding: recap – repeat – give overviews and summaries.

6. **Try** approaches from Kodály, Dalcroze, Suzuki. These aren't always successful, so just give them a go!

7. Remember: dyslexic people can take up to 10 times as long to complete an activity = extra tiredness and perhaps **stress** and poor self-esteem. **Be patient.**

8. Help with **organisation** (in imaginative ways): use mobile phones; post-its; labels; colour-coding; texts. Use written reminders (using large, sans-serif font, if possible, and not handwritten).

9. Consider whether **visual difficulties** could be a problem. Refer to a specialist optometrist if this might be so. This is not a feature of dyslexia but may co-occur. Try copying on to tinted paper (in a colour of the student's choice).

10. Create a supportive, nurturing, safe and compassion-ate environment which allows the student to be their best self.

The Visual Arts

DIANE, do you remember that illustration in Chapter Two of the two sides of the brain? In a person who has dyslexia the right side of the brain, which is responsible for creativity and art, is dominant. This accounts for the high number of successful artists with dyslexia. An artist friend of mine studied fine art at the University of Canterbury in Christchurch. She was impressed that the tutors recognised most of their students had some degree of dyslexia. Hearing that was music to my ears. It certainly was never mentioned when I did my graphic design degree. A large part of my final grade was a dissertation. Several of my classmates ended up with a lower degree than they deserved because no dyslexia support was available to them.

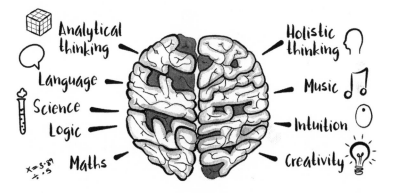

I know very little about the world-building computer game *Minecraft*, but Harry is smitten with it. Without ever reading a manual, he mastered it intuitively. One of the first projects he did when he went to high school was to create a *Minecraft*

world to express his interests. He aced it because he is highly spatially aware. Many people with dyslexia become successful architects. The famous architect Lord Richard Rogers said,

"Dyslexics have a way of looking at problems and turning them on their heads, that's a very exciting way of doing things... you don't accept the standard, because you don't know what the standard is.[70]"

Famous Architects, Artists, Sculptors and Photographers

- Richard Rodgers – Architect
- Norman Foster – Architect
- Auguste Rodin – French Sculptor
- Pablo Picasso – Artist
- Jackson Pollock – Artist
- Chuck Close – Artist
- Andy Warhol – Artist, Director and Film Producer
- Robert Rauschenberg – Pop Artist
- Jeff Thomson – Sculptor who works in corrugated iron
- Rebecca Kamen – Sculptor who is inspired by science
- Gudrun Hasle – Danish Artist who uses spelling mistakes in her art
- Ash Casper – American Designer and Illustrator
- Rachel Deane – American Painter who produces work about shame and trauma
- Leslie Chavez – Photographer

- Michael Shainblum – National Geographic
  Photographer

The Thinker
by Auguste Rodin

You may like to check out painter Gudrun Hasle's work,
in which she makes a feature of misspelt words. Her
paintings remind me of a school project I did in primary
school. I spent days drawing a poster about the Tower
of London. In block capitals above the illustration, I
wrote THE TOWER OF LODON. Unfortunately, I didn't
have Hasle's confidence to call it art. The following is an
excerpt about Hasle's work, taken from *Finding Words
in Paint: How Artists See Dyslexia*.[71]

"I use my dyslexia in everything I do. It's my technique.
It began as an accident. When I started to attend the Art
Academy in Denmark, I painted a painting and added

some texts. I had no time to correct the spelling, so the next day all the other students and professors were trying to read their way through my uncorrected text, and suddenly they were dyslexic. They were having a hard time reading my words. I thought to myself, hmm, this is a very interesting and effective tool. I turned the whole thing around. But it was a giant leap for me to make this change. Since then, I never correct anything. And sometimes the wording is correct – by accident."

Pablo Picasso
Artist

Ways to nurture a child's artistic talent

Encouraging creativity when your child is young can make a difference. Dyslexic Kiwi artist, Jeff Thomson, creates huge sculptures in corrugated iron, but he traces his creative influences back to being taught French knitting, and weaving with flax, as a child.

Rod Judkins, in his book *The Art of Creative Thinking*,[72] uses examples from the lives of famous artists and from his own experience as a tutor at Central Saint Martins Art School in London, to explain how to nurture creativity. Helping a child to develop their creativity means they can try their hand at any number of creative pursuits.

- Make time to visit exhibitions that interest your child
- Sign your child up for an art class
- Ensure they have access to art supplies such as pencils, paints and clay. Don't stop them using paper; it sometimes takes a dozen sheets to get the perfect drawing
- If they have access to a camera, or a phone with a camera, encourage them to take artistic shots and point out good photographs in magazines or exhibitions

Acting

Figuring out how life works is difficult for a person with dyslexia. They constantly watch how other people do things and copy them, so it isn't surprising that acting comes naturally to many dyslexics.

Actor Billy Bob Thornton once said, "I don't think I fit in. I can fit in, but it's like an acting job. Most of my acting is done in public.[73]"

Billy Bob Thornton was severely dyslexic as a child and found school very difficult. In an article on the website Mensjournal.com he is quoted as saying:

> "I was just kind of known around school as a moron. Nobody really encouraged me. Dyslexia drives you, because you're trying to overcome something. They've found that a lot of people with dyslexia and OCD, which I also have, are high achievers in the things like the arts, writing, or whatever, because you compensate in other ways.[74]"

Despite Billy Bob's struggles in school, he became a successful screenwriter. He had his first break when in 1992 he wrote and starred in *One False Move*. Since then, he has written, directed, or acted in multiple films every year, and in 1997 he won an Oscar for his screenwriting.

Famous Actors
- Billy Bob Thornton
- Octavia Spencer
- Danny Glover
- Jay Leno
- Jennifer Aniston
- Jim Carrey
- Keanu Reeves
- Keira Knightley
- Orlando Bloom

- Susan Hampshire
- Tom Cruise
- Vince Vaughn
- Whoopi Goldberg

Whoopi Goldberg
Actor

How to nurture a child's acting ability

Becoming a famous actor is not always about having the most talent. There are stories of well-known actors being discovered by talent scouts as they walked along the street. However, most actors work their way to the top. You can encourage your child's drama ability by:

- Picking a drama class that understands the needs of dyslexic students. Harry found improvisation classes worked best for him, as he can't quickly read pages of a script.

- Suggesting your child participates in drama at school and looking for local amateur dramatic groups which require child actors in their productions. Few movie stars go straight to the big screen; small roles in a local theatre company will provide good acting experience.
- Taking your child to see live theatre and street performances to inspire them.

Science

Carol Greider, who won the Nobel Prize in Medicine for discovering telomerase, an enzyme that has the potential to fight cancer, said she struggled at school with spelling and sounding out words. Seeing her son having similar difficulties, she came to understand that she too had dyslexia. She believes having to work so hard to achieve taught her perseverance.

The fact that people with dyslexia must try so hard and not give up makes them good at dealing with the frustrations of science experiments which often need to be run hundreds of times. The dyslexic ability to think visually is also an advantage in science.

William J. Dreyer, one of the founders of the modern studies in molecular biology, found his ability to visualise reactions occurring on a molecular level was instrumental in his success.

"Dreyer was a classic dyslexic, with the usual reading and

writing problems throughout his early education. Yet, as he struggled through college and graduate school and progressed into laboratory work, he found that he could predict the results of many experiments. He could use his powerful dyslexic imagination to see interactions at the molecular level. Somehow, he was able to visualize the molecules interacting with each other in his head in a way that his non-dyslexic colleagues could not. This gave way to many new theories (in one instance, twelve years ahead of all others in the field) about the links between the human genetic code and the development of the immune system. Later, a different scientist proved experimentally that he was right and received a Nobel Prize.[75]"

Being able to 'see' what other people cannot also helped Dr. Baruj Benacerraf former head of New York's Dana-Farber Cancer Institute and a Nobel Prize winner in immunology. He originally learned of his own dyslexia through the traits diagnosed in his daughter and grandson, and feels he has a better sense of time and three-dimensional space than others in his field due to his dyslexia.[76]

Famous Scientists

- Professor Elizabeth Blackburn – Nobel Prize in Medicine
- Pierre Curie – Scientist
- Michael Faraday – Scientist
- Alexander Graham Bell – Inventor

- Carol W. Greider – Molecular Biologist and Nobel Prize winner
- Dr. Baruj Benacerraf – Immunologist

Ways to nurture a child's scientific interests

Carol W. Greider
Molecular biologist
and Nobel Prize winner

If reading is not an issue for you, there are some good books available on science experiments for children. Harry had one of these books which I read to him. He loved basic experiments such as making vinegar and bicarbonate of soda volcanos. The important thing in developing a love of science is to follow your child's interests.

- I know we sometimes get sick of our children asking *Why?* But encourage your child to ask questions and think critically.
- Allow them to watch science programmes and science

videos on YouTube.

- Younger children are often fascinated by animals or dinosaurs. Allowing them to watch programmes based on their interests or finding good picture books in the local library can foster this interest.

- Find out what holiday programmes your local museum has. Check if they are dyslexic friendly and won't require high-level reading or writing skills.

- Encourage simple experiments at home. While baking and gardening together, create experiments such as how much water different shaped containers can hold, or how tall seeds grow in a week.

Sport

Duncan Goodhew, the British Olympic swimming champion, struggled at school and said his learning difficulties had a terrible impact on his self-esteem.[77]

"Dyslexia made me feel as if I was drowning in the classroom. Competitive swimming was my lifeline. Often dyslexia had made me feel that I had STUPID in neon light flashing on my forehead."

Duncan's unusual appearance didn't help matters. Falling out of a tree at the age of ten triggered alopecia universalis, which left him permanently bald. At thirteen he was diagnosed with dyslexia, and around that time his swimming coach told him he was good enough to swim for his country. He swam in the United States at North Carolina State University while studying for a business degree, and then he swam for Great Britain at the 1976 Montreal Olympics. He didn't achieve any medals at those games but became determined to succeed at the next. At the Moscow Olympics, in 1980, he won a gold medal in the 100-metre breaststroke for Great Britain.

Duncan became a motivational speaker and credited his dyslexia for giving him the drive to excel. He still swims every day and says he finds being in the water a spiritual experience. "For me a one-swim day is a good day, a two-swim day is a great day."

*

Scott Robertson is a former international rugby player playing 23 times for the All Blacks (New Zealand's rugby team) from 1998 to 2002. He is also a top coach, having been appointed as the head coach of the Christchurch based Crusaders team in 2017, and leading them to four consecutive Super Rugby Championships (so far).

Scott has been open about how difficult it has been for him to combat his dyslexia. He scores highly in EQ – emotional intelligence, but often struggles to get his thoughts down on paper.

"I struggle to write an essay – I never was school smart, but I've got good EQ with people, and I've got a good rugby brain. I tried hard at school. I had the work ethic right; I just hadn't found the way that was best for me.[78]"

"It wasn't my strength, any of that kind of stuff; my identity was built around my ability to tackle. That gave me confidence in life."

Like many dyslexics, Scott is a picture thinker. "I am a bullet-point and pictures man. I use pictures so people can get connected - emotionally connected.[79]"

In common with many high-achieving dyslexics, Scott has a supportive partner. He credits his wife, Jane, as being instrumental in his success. "She helped with my dyslexia. She'd look at my work and go 'Holy hell, what have you written here, it's all back to front'. She says, 'just talk' and she writes it... [78]"

Famous Sports People

- Jackie Stewart – Motor Racing Driver
- Duncan Goodhew – Swimmer
- Magic Johnson – Basketball Player
- Meryl Davis – Ice Skater
- Muhammad Ali – Boxer
- Sam Allardyce – UK Footballer and Football Manager
- Jessica Watson – The youngest person to sail solo and unassisted around the world
- Scott Robertson – New Zealand rugby player and coach

How to encourage sporting achievement

As in most things, actions speak louder than words. Being physically active yourself will encourage your child to take sport seriously. However, even if sport is not your thing, you can offer encouragement from the sidelines.

- Teach the value of practice to improve skills and use positive reinforcement to help them develop.
- Celebrate even their small improvements in personal best times. Encourage effort, not success.
- Ask your child what sport they would like to try, and give them the opportunity to dabble in as many sports as possible. Make use of school holiday programmes to try new sports.
- Support their team – go to watch their games and help with fundraising. Behind every great sportsperson is a support crew; family often must make sacrifices to enable their child to reach the top.

Engineering

John Britten was a talented design engineer who lived in Christchurch, New Zealand.[80] Born in 1950, his mother, a teacher, read to him every day throughout his childhood. She couldn't understand when he, unlike his sisters, failed to learn to read and spell. She supported him with his homework but the only subject he excelled in was art.

His father owned a bicycle shop, and John enjoyed helping

him put the bikes together. John loved making things with his hands. One of his first successful projects as a child was a go-cart, which won a race at the Scout Jamboree. He restored an old 'Indian' motorcycle which sparked his lifelong love of bikes. After leaving school, he qualified as a design engineer, and in his spare time he restored an old house, casting the tapware and door handles to his own designs.

The practical skills he learned along the way spurred him on to follow his dream of designing and racing motorbikes. Competing against the world's huge motor-cycle companies, he chose not to modify the design of a conventional motorbike but start afresh, and he came up with a design innovation to reduce the machine's weight; the fuel tank was the bike's seat.

In 1991, his new bike went to race at Daytona in the United States. It made the headlines and was described on the cover of American magazine Cycle World as 'The World's Most Advanced Motorcycle'.

Back in Christchurch, John set up a factory to build his new kind of motorbikes. He also had plans to create a lightweight commuter car and a bicycle powered by wind. Tragically, he was struck down by cancer and died aged forty-five.

John never let his dyslexia hold him back. He followed his dream and became a world leader in the field of motorbike design.

Famous Engineers

- Henry Ford – Founder of the Ford Motor Company and developer of the first assembly line for mass production
- The Wright Brothers – Orville and Wilbur Wright were the creators of the first plane and made their first flight in 1903
- Maggie Aderin-Pocock – Mechanical Engineer and Space Scientist
- John Britten – Motorbike Designer

Henry Ford
Car manufacturer

How to encourage engineering skills

There are many different fields of engineering. I wasn't surprised when my nephew became a successful civil engineer. As a child, he spent every weekend, and much of the school holidays, digging huge holes at the beach.

The following tips are taken from the Hechinger Report.[81]

- Give children toys that have "manipulative elements" like balls and rattles. Ask children to control elements of these toys, like building higher towers or making the rattle softer or louder.
- Have children explain how simple tools work, like a can opener or a door hinge.
- Allow infants to practice "repetitive play", like dropping a spoon over and over, which helps the child learn about concepts like gravity long before they know what gravity is.
- Give children time to practice four kinds of play: pretend play that involves a child using their imagination; exploratory play where children create experiments or take things apart; guided play where adults play and interact with children, and free play without an adult involved.
- Allow exploratory play (within reason and with safety in mind), even if that means a toddler may get dirty.
- Ask "why", "what" and "how" questions as much as possible to push children to explain their thinking.
- Use complex and accurate vocabulary words, even with babies. Introduce them to words like "stable" when building a tower or "fragile" when touching objects.
- Teach children that they are constantly learning by encouraging them to say, "I can't do this yet" instead of "I can't do this".

Entrepreneurship

A word impossible for a dyslexic person to spell is entrepreneur. It comes from the French word entreprendre meaning 'to undertake'. Many dyslexic people are natural entrepreneurs. According to the Oxford dictionary, an entrepreneur is 'A person who sets up a business or businesses, taking on financial risks in the hope of profit'.

"Entrepreneurship is the ability to recognize the bigger picture, find where there's an opportunity to make someone's life better, design hypotheses around these opportunities and continually test your assumptions. It's experimentation: Some experiments will work; many others will fail. It is not big exits, huge net worth or living a life of glamour. It's hard work and persistence to leave the world a better place once your time here is done." – Konrad Billetz, co-founder and co-CEO of Offset Solar.[82]

Julie Logan, Emeritus Professor of Entrepreneurship at Cass Business School, in London, says that 20% of the UK's business self-starters have dyslexia, and in the US the figure is as high as 35%. People with dyslexia often prefer to work for themselves because when they are their own boss, they can create a working environment that suits their skills and supports their weaknesses.[83]

Josh Almeida, an audio/visual entrepreneur, gave a PechaKucha talk entitled 'The Power of Dyslexia', on how he overcame his dyslexia to succeed.[84] In it, he says, "To innovate you have to know how to fail." As a dyslexic person, Josh knew all about failure from his difficulties at school. He was held back a year at primary school and ended up in the special education class because of his inability to read. Josh grew up in Orlando, going to theme parks as often as possible. He loved the fantasy world these parks created and set his heart on working in the audio-visual industry. Eventually, through hard work, he was offered a job as a Disney Imagineer but decided to turn down the opportunity and set up his own audio-visual business Ascend Studios. His company has worked for The Ritz-Carlton Hotel Company, Loews Hotels and Universal Studios. He attributes his success to his dyslexia, which has made him highly creative with excellent spatial awareness.

*

The Prince of Wales knighted Richard Branson, the world's most famous dyslexic entrepreneur, for his services to entrepreneurship. As a young child, Richard had speech problems and some coordination difficulties. He was sent to a boarding school when he was eight years old and hated it. He couldn't read or spell and was frequently beaten. He found a way to achieve was by being good at sports, and he became the captain of the football, rugby and cricket teams. However, a football injury snatched this success away from him. When Richard was eleven, he set up a business in the school holidays breeding budgerigars. His father built an aviary for them, and the birds bred faster than he could sell them. This gave him a taste for business.

He established a magazine called *The Student* and dropped every subject except ancient history to devote all his time to it. He left school at sixteen, and his headmaster's parting words were: "Congratulations, Branson. I predict you will either go to prison or become a millionaire."

Richard Branson
Entrepreneur

Running the magazine led Richard to meet many pop stars of his day. He decided to sell mail-order pop records through the magazine, and a friend suggested he rename the magazine *Virgin* as they were virgins at business. The *Virgin* brand went on to set up *Virgin Megastores* and diversify into numerous other fields.

Richard Branson is one of the wealthiest people in the UK, with a net worth estimated at over three billion pounds. He now has his sights set on space travel with Virgin Galactic.[85]

Famous Entrepreneurs

- Charles Schwab – Financial Executive
- Craig McCaw – Cellular Phone Pioneer
- Richard Branson – Business Magnate
- David Neeleman – Founder of Jet Blue Airways
- Anita Roddick - Founder of The Body Shop
- Jamie Oliver – Chef
- Ingvar Kamprad – Founder of IKEA

How to encourage entrepreneurship in your child

- Children need entrepreneurial examples. You may not be an entrepreneur, but who do you know with their own business? Would they be a suitable entrepreneurial mentor for your child? As a teen, Harry's cousin, Sam had an online clothing store. Sam was into skateboarding and designed cool streetwear tops and T-shirts. He was an excellent entrepreneurial example for Harry. By connecting your child to an entrepreneur, you make entrepreneurship seem possible.

- People with dyslexia are good at failing and entrepreneurs need this skill. Their first business idea will rarely be successful. By sharing stories of your failures, you demonstrate that failing is a normal part of life. Perfectionism is crippling, and children need to know how to cope when things don't work out. For a child to make it as an entrepreneur, they must be comfortable with failing and see it as a necessary part of learning.

- Passion, not money drives successful entrepreneurs. Getting your child to brainstorm what they care about should be the starting point of developing their business idea. Like Harry's cousin, Sam, with his clothing brand, children will enjoy a business they care passionately about.

- As a child, my brother bred stick insects and sold them to his friends. He was a natural entrepreneur. At an age-appropriate level, children can have a business; be it a stall outside the gate, babysitting or dog walking. Activities such as these teach useful business skills, including communication and marketing.

- The next generation of entrepreneurs needs creative thinkers. Encourage your child's crazy dreams, then help them find practical applications by asking, "Who are your customers?"

Top Tip 10

Identify your child's strengths and build on them.

Top Fact 10

Children with dyslexia are often strong in the fields of the arts, science, sport, architecture, engineering and entrepreneurship.

Chapter Eight

Oh, the lengths you'll go to

That's a Wrap

We'd better wrap up this conversation at the school gate, DIANE. I must get Harry to football training. It's been good chatting with you. I hope you found my tips helpful. I appreciate it's a lot to take in, and I know that some information may not apply to your child, so thanks for bearing with me.

It is hard when your precious child starts at school and suddenly runs into the roadblock called literacy. Primary school is all about reading and writing. Every day our kids experience failure, and it is heartbreaking to watch them suffer, but I hope this book has given you hope that there are ways you can help your child succeed. Becoming their cheerleader is your key role. Continue to pour your unconditional love into their love tank. I know some days you will wish you could walk away. It takes tremendous perseverance to fight for the help your child requires.

If you also have non-dyslexic children, they may tell you that you favour your dyslexic child because you give them so much more attention. Don't beat yourself up. I believe this is inevitable; a child with learning needs requires more parental support.

The mountain of dyslexia is a tough one to climb, but with your support your child is off to great places.

I have focused much of this book on the early years of a child's life. That is because I believe getting a diagnosis and putting support in place as early as possible will make a difference to your child. However, don't be discouraged if your child's dyslexia was not picked up early. I was an adult before I recognised my dyslexia. Accepting it has made a huge difference to my life. I feel free to hold my head up high and own my dumb mistakes without feeling ashamed. I have put a support group in place to help me accomplish my writing goals. I now see dyslexia as a strength and not a weakness – it has given me my gift of creativity.

I hope you will investigate the health issues I have

highlighted, particularly the link with gluten intolerance/ coeliac disease and fatty acid deficiency. I cannot stress enough how important it is to take this seriously.

Likewise, identifying other learning challenges such as ADD, or dyscalculia will make a huge difference to your child. Understanding why they struggle with certain things helps lift their mantel of shame and enables you to accept they aren't naughty or irritating for the sake of it.

If your child appears to have multiple issues, you may wish to get a formal diagnosis carried out by a registered C-grade tester. This will identify the specific help they require.

I know parenting a child with learning difficulties can be overwhelming. I hope you have made notes about what applies to your situation. If not, flick back through the book and write a list of things you would like to tackle. Tick them off one at a time.

Remember, helping your child is a marathon, not a sprint. Children can only learn when they are ready. If you hit a roadblock, move to the next item and return to the other one later.

I'm aware that many of the suggestions in this book come with a price tag. Getting a full assessment is expensive, but there is no need to go straight there. I recommend initially checking out the online assessment tools. You may like to try the test on nessy.com under the heading About Dyslexia http://dyslexiatest.me/

I mentioned earlier in the book that I'd probably missed some things Harry tried when he was younger. I now recall he used https://www.nessy.com/uk/product/nessy-fingers/ to improve his touch typing. Nessy.com has a range of excellent low-cost resources on their website.

Here is a list of other low-cost ways you can help your child.

- Visit your local library. Ask what resources they have to help children with dyslexia
- Read the websites mentioned in this book
- Join Facebook groups for home-schooling parents. You can often pick up quality second-hand resources from such groups
- Work closely with the Head of Learning Support at your child's school to ensure your child is getting as much support as possible
- If grandparents ask for gift ideas for birthday or Christmas and are able to afford this, suggest a term of tutoring for your child

My 10 Top Tips

1. Ask your doctor to check your child for glue ear if you suspect it may be an issue.

2. If your child can't recognise the sounds in words, take them for a hearing test. If this is normal, investigate for

phonological challenges such as auditory processing disorder.

3. Have your child's vision checked by a behavioural optometrist for Irlen Syndrome and investigate the *Schoolvision* checks.

4. If working memory is a problem for your child, play memory games with them.

5. Make sleep a priority for your child.

6. Invest in whatever additional learning support school can offer and, if necessary, top up with whatever tuition you can afford.

7. If you suspect there is more than dyslexia holding your child back, have them tested for additional learning challenges such as ADD.

8. Investigate if food intolerances may be an issue for your child.

9. Be aware of a dyslexic child's vulnerability to abuse and teach them how to stay safe in the real world and online.

10. Identify your child's strengths and passions and build on them.

Don't forget about the success attributes that the Frostig Center uncovered.

- **Self-awareness** – don't let your child be defined by what they can't do.
- **Proactivity** – help your child to understand they have the power to control their own destiny.
- **Perseverance** – teach your child to find their way around obstacles and to be flexible when necessary.
- **Goal Setting** – model how to set concrete, realistic and achievable goals for your child.
- **Presence and Use of Effective Social Support Systems** – help your child to develop a support system, and as they mature encourage independence.
- **Emotional Stability** – teach your child how to recognise emotional triggers and develop coping strategies such as maintaining good peer relationships and being socially active.

*

I hope reading through the list of successful people who have overcome dyslexia was encouraging for you and your child. These people were in your child's shoes once upon a time, struggling to get through school.

The mountain of dyslexia is tough to climb, but with your support, your child is off to great places. By focusing on their strengths, and being there to encourage them, who knows what your child will accomplish?

I hope we bump into each other again at this school gate. I can't wait to hear how you are getting on.

DIANE, it's been good spending time with you. I trust you've enjoyed it too. Before you go, can I ask for a special favour? I'd appreciate it if you would leave a review wherever you bought this book.

Book reviews help to sell books. I'm on a quest to get 500 reviews, and I can only do it with your help.

How to submit your review.

Go to the platform where you purchased this book.

1. Type into the search bar, Dyslexia. Wrestling with an Octopus.

2. Click on the book.

3. Scroll down the page to where you see 'Customer reviews'. There may be a chart showing 1-5 star reviews.

4. Beneath the chart, click on the box that says, 'Write a customer review.'

5. Add your review. It doesn't have to be very long; just say what you enjoyed about the book. If you have a specific comment, rather than posting a harsh review, please email me at hello@dyslexiaoctopus.com

6. Click submit.

I'd also love it if you could tell any of your friends who may be interested in this book about it via your social media pages.

It has been a pleasure spending time with you. To continue this conversation, go to www.dyslexiaoctopus.com

All the best!

Acknowledgements

This book has been a labour of love over many years. I have updated Harry's age on these pages numerous times. I want to thank my family for their patience while I worked on this manuscript. I would also like to thank Kate Beadle and Belinda O'Keefe for their editing skills, and my fabulous niece, Sinéad Doherty, for the hours she spent formatting this book. Additional thanks go to Asher Olliver, Lily Holliday and my husband, Simon, for their help with editing, web design and marketing.

To my wonderful son, Harry, we have been on quite a journey – I have learned so much about my dyslexia as I sought to help you. I have no doubt you will accomplish great things. As Dr Seuss put it – Oh, the places you'll go!

Bibliography

[1] Geisel T (1995). The Secret Art of Dr. Seuss. Random House. ISBN13: 9780679434481.

[2] Dyslexia Foundation New Zealand (n.d.). Unlocking dyslexia: making good in the youth justice system. https://www.dyslexiafoundation.org.nz/dyslexia_advocacy/justice.php. Accessed 25 August 2020.

[3] Hughes N, Williams H, Chitsabesan P, Davies R and Mounce L (2012). Nobody Made the Connection: The Prevalence of Neurodisability in young people who offend. Report for the UK's Children's Commissioner report. https://www.childrenscommissioner.gov.uk/report/nobody-made-the-connection/

[4] Rose J (2009). Identifying and teaching children and young people with dyslexia and literacy difficulties. An independent report for the UK Department for Children, Schools and Families (DCSF). https://dera.ioe.ac.uk//14790/

[5] Snow CE, Burns MS & Griffin P (eds) (1998). Preventing Reading Difficulties in Young Children. Washington, DC: The

National Academies Press. https://doi.org/10.17226/6023

[6] Fletcher JM, Lyon GR, Fuchs LS, Barnes MA (2007. Learning disabilities: From identification to intervention. The Guilford Press; New York, London. https://eric.ed.gov/?id=ED492950

[7] APPG (2019). Educational cost of dyslexia: Financial, standards and attainment cost to education of unidentified and poorly supported dyslexia, and a policy pathway to end the educational cost of dyslexia. Report from the All-Party Parliamentary Group for Dyslexia and other SpLDs. https://archive.ph/TmDbT

[8] Dyslexia Research Institute (n.d.) Resources. http://archive.today/hcoiV

[9] Schumacher J, Hoffmann P, Schmäl C, Schulte Körne G & Nöthen MM (2007). Genetics of dyslexia: The evolving landscape. Journal of Medical Genetics, 44(5), 289–297. https://doi.org/10.1136/jmg.2006.046516

[10] Bragonier D (2015) The True Gifts of a Dyslexic Mind. TEDx Talk. https://youtu.be/_dPyzFFcG7A

[11] Sherman G (2004). Dr. Gordon Sherman on Brain Research and Reading. http://impactofspecialneeds.weebly.com/uploads/3/4/1/9/3419723/brain_research_and_reading.pdf
https://www.greatschools.org/gk/articles/structural-brain-differences-in-kids-with-dyslexia/

[12] Dyslexia Victoria (n.d.). Dyslexic problems & traits in children and adults. http://dyslexiavictoriaonline.com/dyslexic-yslexic-problems-traits-in-children-adults/. Accessed 25 August 2020.

[13] van der Leij A (2013). Dyslexia and Early Intervention: What Did We Learn from the Dutch Dyslexia Programme?. Dyslexia, 19: 241-255. https://doi.org/10.1002/dys.1466

[14] Gillon G (2017). The effectiveness of phonological awareness instruction to enhance early literacy success for young children most at risk. American Speech-Language Hearing Association Annual Convention, 9-11 Nov 2017. Los Angeles, CA. https://www.canterbury.ac.nz/media/documents/education-and-health/gail-gillon---phonological-awareness-resources/conference--workshop-handouts/ASHA-2017-PowerPoint-Slides.pdf Accessed November 23, 2020

[15] Bright Solutions (2014). What is Dyslexia? Retrieved April 14, 2020, from https://dys-add.com/dyslexia.html#anchorResearchNIH1994

[16] Neufeld G & Maté G (2006). Hold on to Your Kids: Why Parents Need to Matter More Than Peers. 0375760288 (ISBN13: 9780375760280).

[17] Peer L (2009). Dyslexia and glue ear: A sticky educational problem. In Reid G (Ed) The Routledge

Companion to Dyslexia. Routledge. https://doi.org/10.4324/9780203549230

[18] Valentino RL (2009). Chronic dysfunction of the eustachian tube. https://www.clinicaladvisor.com/home/features/chronic-dysfunction-of-the-eustachian-tube/

[19] Peer L & Reid G (eds) (2016) Multilingualism, Literacy and Dyslexia: Breaking down barriers for educators (2nd edition). Routledge.

[20] South Island Alliance (2011). Middle ear conditions: Otitis media and grommets. In The Health Status of Children and Young People in the South Island 2011, pages 197-214. South Island Alliance.

[21] Marshall A (2013) The Everything Parent's Guide to Children with Dyslexia. (2nd edition). Adams Media Corporation.

[22] Hafner K (2018). The Couple Who Helped Decode Dyslexia. The New York Times. https://archive.ph/0IrE5

[23] Winter L (2020). How is a phonogram different from a phoneme? https://archive.ph/mCkTE

[24] Hallowell EM & Ratey JJ (2006). Delivered from Distraction: Getting the Most Out of Life with Attention Deficit Disorder. Ballantine Books Trade Paperback Edition.

[25] Irlen (2014). Do I Have Dyslexia or Irlen Syndrome?

https://irlen.com/the-difference-between-irlen-syndrome-and-visual-dyslexia/. Accessed August 25 2020.

[26] Knebel C (2016). Sleep deprived dyslexic. https://blog.dyslexia.com/sleep-deprived-dyslexic/. Accessed May 15 2020.

[27] Foss B (2016). The Dyslexia Empowerment Plan; a blueprint for renewing your child's confidence and love of learning. Ballantine Books. ISBN 9780345541253.

[28] Davis RD with Braun EM (2010). The Gift of Dyslexia: Why Some of the Smartest People Can't Read...and How They Can Learn. ISBN: 978-0399535666. https://www.dyslexia.com/book/the-gift-of-dyslexia/

[29] Sascentre. (n.d.). Ear Dominance. https://www.sascentre.com/bulletin/171-ear-dominance. Accessed April 15 2020.

[30] Tomatis AA (1991). The Conscious Ear: My Life of Transformation Through Listening. N.Y. Station Hill Press.

[31] Buzan T, (2018). Mind Map Mastery: The Complete Guide to Learning and Using the Most Powerful Thinking Tool in the Universe. https://ebooksbag.com/pdf-epub-mind-map-mastery-the-complete-guide-to-learning-and-using-the-most-powerful-thinking-tool-in-the-universe-download/

[32] Cicerchia M (n.d.) 5 Types of learning difficulties. https://www.readandspell.com/types-of-learning-difficulties#. Accessed May 14 2020.

[33] International Dyslexia Association (n.d.). Attention-Deficit/Hyperactivity Disorder (AD/HD) and Dyslexia. https://dyslexiaida.org/attention-deficithyperactivity-disorder-adhd-and-dyslexia/. Accessed May 14 2020.

[34] Amen D (2013). Healing ADD from the inside out: the breakthrough program that allows you to see and heal the 7 types of ADD. Berkley Books, New York.

[35] Sharma M, Purdy SC & Kelly AS (2009) Comorbidity of Auditory Processing, Language, and Reading Disorders appears in Journal of Speech, Language, and Hearing Research Vol 52 pages 706-722 https://doi.org/10.1044/1092-4388(2008/07-0226)

[36] Dewey D (1995). What Is Developmental Dyspraxia? Brain and Cognition Volume 29, Issue 3, Pages 254-274. https://doi.org/10.1006/brcg.1995.1281

[37] Based on Cicerchia M (n.d.) 7 Dysgraphia symptoms in children. https://www.readandspell.com/dysgraphia-symptoms-in-children. Accessed May 14 2020.

[38] Dyslexia and Mathematics https://archive.ph/snflB

[39] Attebery L (n.d.). Diane Swonk, Founder of Diane Swonk Economics. http://dyslexia.yale.edu/story/diane-swonk/. Accessed May 14 2020.

[40] Rippel M (n.d.). How Making Connections Helps Your Child's Memory. Free E-Book https://bit.ly/3chYYdq Affiliate

link

[41] Farkas RD (2003). Effects of Traditional versus Learning-Styles Instructional Methods on Middle School Students. The Journal of Educational Research 97, 1, 42–51. https://www.jstor.org/stable/27542462

[42] Powers NR, Eicher JD, Butter F, Kong Y, Miller LL, Ring SM, Mann M & Gruen JR (2013). Alleles of a Polymorphic ETV6 Binding Site in DCDC2 Confer Risk of Reading and Language Impairment. The American Journal of Human Genetics, 93, 1, 19–28. https://doi.org/10.1016/j.ajhg.2013.05.0084

[43] Dyslexia Research Trust (n.d.). Immunological Factors in Dyslexia. https://www.dyslexic.org.uk/immunological-factors. Accessed June 9 2019.

[44] Sciurti M, Fornaroli F, Gaiani F, Bonaguri C, Leandro G, Di Mario F & De' Angelis GL (2018). Genetic susceptibility and celiac disease: what role do HLA haplotypes play?. Acta bio-medica : Atenei Parmensis, 89, (9-S), 17–21. https://doi.org/10.23750/abm.v89i9-s.7953

[45] Coeliac UK (2020). Coeliac UK 2020-2025 Strategy. https://www.coeliac.org.uk/document-library/6745-coeliac-uk-2020-2025-strategy/coeliac-uk-2020-2025-strategy.pdf. Accessed August 25 2020.

[46] Knivsberg A-M (1997) Urine patterns, peptide levels and IgA/IgG antibodies to food proteins in children with

dyslexia. Pediatric Rehabilitation 1, 1, 25-33. https://doi.org/10.3109/17518429709060939

[47] Singh P, Arora A, Strand TA, Leffler DA, Catassi C, Green PH, Kelly CP, Ahuja V, & Makharia GK (2018). Global Prevalence of Celiac Disease: Systemic Review and meta-analysis. Clinical Gastroenterology and Hepatology 16, 823–836. https://doi.org/10.1016/j.cgh.2017.06.037

[48] Hugdahl K, Synnevåg B & Satz P (1990). Immune and autoimmune diseases in dyslexic children [published correction appears in Neuropsychologia 1991;29, 2, 211]. Neuropsychologia 28, 7, 673-679. doi:10.1016/0028-3932(90)90122-5

[49] Not T, Horvath K, Hill ID, Fasano A, Hammed A & Magazzu G (1996). Endomysium antibodies in blood donors predicts a high prevalence of celiac disease in the USA. Gastroenterology 110, A351.

[50] Coeliac UK (n.d.). Help us diagnose more people. https://www.coeliac.org.uk/get-involved/campaign-with-us/help-us-diagnose-more-people/. Accessed August 25 2020.

[51] Gluten-Free Living (2018). What Is Gluten Sensitivity? https://www.glutenfreeliving.com/gluten-free/gluten-sensitivity/what-is-gluten-sensitivity/ Accessed April 16, 2020.

[52] Richardson AJ, Calvin CM, Clisby C, Schoenheimer DR, Montgomery P, Hall JA, Hebb G, Westwood E, Talcott

JB & Stein JF (2000). Fatty acid deficiency signs predict the severity of reading and related difficulties in dyslexic children. Prostaglandins, Leukotrienes and Essential Fatty Acids 63, 1, 69–74. https://doi.org/10.1054/plef.2000.0194

[53] Wahls T (2014). Could Vegetarianism Increase Your Risk of Autoimmune Disease? https://www.mindbodygreen.com/0-13007/could-vegetarianism-increase-your-risk-of-autoimmune-disease.html Accessed May 16, 2019,

[54] Rucklidge JJ, Eggleston MJ, Johnstone JM, Darling K & Frampton CM (2018). Vitamin mineral treatment improves aggression and emotional regulation in children with ADHD: a fully blinded, randomized, placebo controlled trial. J Child Psychol Psychiatr, 59: 232-246. https://doi.org/10.1111/jcpp.12817

[55] Hardman PK & Morton DG (1991). The link between developmental dyslexia, ADD and chemical dependency. Environmental Medicine 8, 3, 61-72.

[56] McCormick N (2007). How I dragged myself back. https://archive.ph/CoSyN

[57] Hirschman D (2010). Your brain on drugs: dopamine and addiction. https://bigthink.com/going-mental/your-brain-on-drugs-dopamine-and-addiction.

[58] Ryan M & International Dyslexia Association (2004). Social and Emotional Problems Related to Dyslexia I, http://www.ldonline.org/article/19296/. Accessed April 16, 2020

[59] Ryan M (2004). Unlocking the Social and Emotional Enigmas of Dyslexia, Perspectives, 30, No. 4, 1-4.

[60] Griffiths M (1993). Self-identity and Self-esteem: achieving equality in education, Oxford Review of Education 19, 3, 301-317. https://doi.org/10.1080/0305498930190304

[61] McWilliams J (2016). Dyslexia and Intimate Relationships: Disconnection, disunion or a call to embrace difference? A research portfolio submitted in partial fulfilment for the requirements for the degree Master of Counselling. University of Auckland. https://www.janekjersten.co.nz/pdfs/dyslexia-and-intimate-relationships.pdf

[62] McCormack B (1991) Sexual abuse and learning disabilities; another iceberg. British Medical Journal 303, 143-144. https://doi.org/10.1136/bmj.303.6795.143.

[63] Fuller-Thomson E, Carroll SZ & Yang W (2018). Suicide attempts among individuals with specific learning disorders: An under-recognized issue. Journal of Learning Disabilities, 51(3), 283–292. https://doi.org/10.1177/0022219417714776

[64] Elliott L & O'Brien W (2014) Loves Me Not. Random House.

[65] Goldberg RJ, Higgins EL, Raskind MH & Herman KL (2003). Predictors of Success in Individuals with Learning Disabilities: A Qualitative Analysis of a 20-Year Longitudinal Study. Learning Disabilities Research and Practice 18, 4,

222–236. https://doi.org/10.1111/1540-5826.00077

[66] Frostig Center (2009). The 6 Success Factors for Children with Learning Disabilities: Ready-To-Use Activities to Help Kids with LD Succeed in School and in Life. Jossey-Bass. ISBN13: 9780470383773.

[67] Chapman G & Campbell R (2016). The 5 Love Languages of Children: the secret to loving children effectively. Northfield Publishing. B01BXPWGX4 Excerpts from Pages 17-20

[68] Eide BL & Eide FF (2011). The Dyslexic Advantage: Unlocking the Hidden Potential of the Dyslexic Brain. Hudson Street Press. ISBN13: 9781594630798.

[69] British Dyslexia Association (n.d.). Music and dyslexia. https://archive.ph/mck6a

[70] The Yale Centre for Dyslexia & Creativity (n.d.) Richard Rogers, Architect. https://dyslexia.yale.edu/story/richard-rogers/. Accessed April 17 2020.

[71] Johnson LA (2017). Finding Words in Paint: How Artists See Dyslexia. https://www.npr.org/sections/ed/2017/01/25/507405986/finding-words-in-paint-how-artists-see-dyslexia. Accessed 25 August 2020.

[72] Judkins R (2016). The Art of Creative Thinking: 89 Ways to See Things Differently. TarcherPerigee. ISBN13: 9780399176838.

[73] D'Agostino R (2009) Esquire the Meaning of Life: Wisdom, Humor, and Damn Good Advice from 64 Extraordinary Lives. Hearst.

[74] Woods S (n.d.). Billy Bob Thornton on Aging, Overcoming Dyslexia, and the Value of Religion. https://www.mensjournal.com/entertainment/billy-bob-thornton-on-aging-overcoming-dyslexia-and-the-value-of-religion/ Accessed April 14 2020.

[75] West TG (2014). "Amazing Shortcomings, Amazing Strengths": Beginning to Understand the Hidden Talents of Dyslexics. Asia Pacific Journal of Developmental Differences 1, 78-89). https://www.das.org.sg/images/publications/apjdd/apjddjan2014/APJDDVol1No1-west.pdf

[76] West TG (2005) The Gifts of Dyslexia: Talents Among Dyslexics and Their Families. Hong Kong Journal of Paediatrics 10, 153-158. http://www.hkjpaed.org/pdf/2005;10;153-158.pdf

[77] Dyslexia.com (n.d.) Duncan Goodhew – swimmer, Olympic medallist. https://www.dyslexia.com/famous/duncan-goodhew/ Accessed April 17, 2020.

[78] New Zealand Herald (2017). Razor beats dyslexia in coaching climb. https://www.nzherald.co.nz/sport/news/article.cfm?c_id=4&objectid=11928296. Accessed 25 August 2020.

[79] Knowler R (2017) Crusaders coach Scott Robertson talks

about beating dyslexia and the adrenaline of coaching. https://www.stuff.co.nz/sport/rugby/super-rugby/99432266/crusaders-boss-scott-robertson-talks-about-beating-dyslexia-and-the-adrenaline-of-coaching. Accessed 25 August 2020.

[80] Beck J (2004). John Britten - The Boy Who Did Do Better. Scholastic NZ Limited. ISBN: 9781869435486

[81] Mader J, 2018, Eight ways to introduce kids to STEM at an early age. https://hechingerreport.org/eight-ways-introduce-young-kids-stem-early-age/. Accessed May 14 2020.

[82] Freedman M (2020. Entrepreneurship Defined: What It Means to Be an Entrepreneur. Business News daily. https://archive.ph/QT9dv

[83] Tickle L (2015) Dyslexic entrepreneurs – why they have a competitive edge. The Guardian. https://www.theguardian.com/small-business-network/2015/jan/15/dyslexic-entrepreneurs-competitive-edge-business-leaders

[84] Almeida J (2018). The power of dyslexia. Josh Almeida - PKN Orlando v22. https://www.youtube.com/watch?v=X6CSrkuZhAU. Accessed April 17 2020

[85] Based on Astrum people (n.d.). Richard Branson biography: Success story of Virgin Group founder. https://astrumpeople.com/richard-branson-biography/ Accessed April 1, 2020.